JULIAN DELPHIKI

UPDATED EDITION

OPTIMIZING SEO AND PAID SEARCH FUNDAMENTALS

Search

OPTIMIZING SEO AND PAID SEARCH FUNDAMENTALS

Master your content strategy and develop your online video marketing

- Julian Delphiki -

Optimizing SEO and paid search fundamentals / Julian Delphiki – 1st Edition

ISBN 9798647414281

INDEX

TESTING AND OPTIMIZATION

INTRO ABOUT THE NEW EDITION

I am thrilled to present to you the latest edition of Search fundamentals. Over the years, your support and feedback have been invaluable in shaping the evolution of this book. In this new edition, I am excited to share with you some significant updates and improvements that I believe will enhance your reading experience and provide even greater value.

The most notable change in this new edition is the addition of an entirely new three chapters. These chapters has been included at the very beginning of the book due to its utmost importance in setting the tone for what follows. It serves as a gateway to the world of knowledge and insights that this book offers. This new chapter represents fresh perspectives, recent research findings like the leak documents regarding Google algorithm, new forms of search (video search and circle search), AI in SEO, and latest news like the partnership between Reddit and Google and the implications for SEO.

Most notably, the technology that has had the most profound impact on the content of this book in recent years is not voice search, as was the trend a few years back, but the release and widespread adoption of generative AI. This transformative technology has revolutionized how we approach and understand various aspects of our field, and its influence is evident throughout the pages of this edition.

But that is not all; every other chapter in the book has also undergone thorough review and revision to ensure that the content remains up-to-date and aligned with the latest advancements in the field. I have worked diligently to incorporate the most recent research, trends, and practical insights to provide you with the most current and comprehensive information available. This meticulous review process ensures that the book continues to be a reliable and relevant resource for you, regardless of whether you are a student, a professional, or a curious enthusiast.

I want to extend my heartfelt gratitude to all of you who have supported this book throughout its journey. Your enthusiasm and engagement have inspired me to strive for excellence in each edition, and I hope this latest edition continues to meet and exceed your expectations.

As you embark on this renewed journey through the pages of Search fundamentals, I invite you to immerse yourself in the new chapter and explore the refined content within. I am confident that the knowledge and insights you gain from this edition will empower you on your own journeys, both personal and professional

UPDATE

STATE OF SEARCH WITH GENERATIVE AI

GENERATIVE AI

In the ever-evolving landscape of digital marketing, staying ahead of the curve is not just a preference, but a necessity. As the digital realm continues to expand, so do the tools and technologies that shape how businesses connect with their audience. One such transformative force that has emerged in recent years is Artificial Intelligence (AI), a field that has penetrated various industries, and notably, has begun to revolutionize the way Search Engine Optimization (SEO) and Search Engine Marketing (SEM) strategies are conceptualized and executed.

This chapter embarks on an exploration of this exciting juncture where AI, particularly ChatGPT, intersects with the dynamic domain of SEO and SEM. ChatGPT, a product of the cutting-edge GPT-3.5 architecture developed by OpenAI, represents a milestone in natural language processing. It is not just a tool; It is a digital collaborator that can understand, generate, and manipulate human-like text. With capabilities ranging from drafting emails to generating code, ChatGPT's potential reaches far and wide.

For digital marketing professionals, whether they are spearheading campaigns for established corporations or innovative startups, understanding how AI can augment their strategies is a pivotal step towards sustainable success. This chapter aims to demystify the realm of AI in the context of SEO and SEM, focusing on how ChatGPT, as a prominent AI model, can be harnessed to enhance marketing endeavors.

As we delve deeper, we will uncover the multifaceted ways in which ChatGPT can reshape SEO and SEM landscapes. From automating routine tasks like content creation and keyword optimization to deciphering user intent and generating compelling ad copy, ChatGPT's versatility offers a spectrum of possibilities. However, with great power comes responsibility. Alongside the benefits lie challenges and risks, from maintaining authenticity in generated content to ethical considerations about data usage and privacy.

The dawn of AI in SEO and SEM not only brings challenges but also opens up new vistas of opportunity. By embracing AI, digital marketers can unlock unprecedented efficiency, enabling them to focus on strategic decision-making rather than mundane tasks. Yet, as we tread this transformative path, It is essential to remain cognizant of the potential pitfalls and tread carefully to strike the right balance between human ingenuity and AI prowess.

In the chapters that follow, we will dissect the inner workings of ChatGPT, explore real-world applications of AI in SEO and SEM, and delve into strategies for seamlessly integrating AI-powered solutions into existing marketing frameworks. By the end of this journey, you will be equipped with the knowledge and insights to harness the AI revolution, adapting it to your unique marketing endeavors while navigating the challenges that lie ahead.

A THREAT FOR GOOGLE (IN AN UNEXPECTED WAY)

At its core, OpenAI's ambition with ChatGPT Search is revolutionary: to replace Google's ubiquitous search engine with an AI-powered alternative. Leveraging its advanced language model, ChatGPT, OpenAI aims to create a conversational search experience that delivers precise and useful results.

Unlike traditional search engines, where algorithms determine the relevance of results, ChatGPT Search takes a different approach. It scours the vast expanse of the internet in real-time, using natural language processing to understand user queries and provide tailored responses.

Imagine wanting to make lasagna but only having a few ingredients on hand. With ChatGPT Search, you can engage in a conversation with the AI, explaining your culinary desires and ingredient constraints. The AI then searches through countless online recipes to curate a selection that fits your needs. This contextual understanding and personalized search capability set ChatGPT Search apart from competitors, offering a truly bespoke experience.

According to Bloomberg, ChatGPT Search will integrate seamlessly into the existing ChatGPT platform, offering advanced functionalities like citation generation. This enhancement signals OpenAI's commitment to improving the accuracy and utility of its chatbot responses, addressing user feedback, and iterating on its initial offerings.

Reports from The Information suggest that ChatGPT Search may leverage technology powered by Bing, hinting at a potential collaboration that could significantly boost its search capabilities. By partnering with industry leaders, OpenAI aims to deliver a search engine that not only rivals but surpasses existing standards of functionality and efficiency.

ChatGPT is a type of generative AI known as a large language model, defined by its ability to answer questions in plain English. For example, when planning a winter vacation to Europe, I asked ChatGPT for recommendations. It provided eight cities, explaining the pros and cons of each. I then inquired about Innsbruck, one of the suggested cities. ChatGPT informed me about Innsbruck's excellent skiing, Christmas markets, and coffee houses, while noting that some tourists prefer more remote alpine villages and that Innsbruck can be expensive.

My search was completed in seconds, providing instant, connected, and friendly answers without the need to scroll through multiple Google results.

This innovation represents a significant threat to Google. A New York Times article described it as a "code red" moment for Google, highlighting ChatGPT's unsuitability for delivering digital ads, which constitute 80% of Google's revenue.

Initially, Google executives dismissed the threat, citing "reputational risk" in developing a ChatGPT rival. However, on February 7th, the same day Microsoft announced Bing's integration with a more powerful AI technology from OpenAI, Google revealed Bard, its own generative AI solution, which would enter semi-public beta testing immediately.

CHATGPT APPLICATIONS IN SEO

In the dynamic landscape of digital marketing, the ability to adapt swiftly and scale efficiently is paramount. Enter Generative Artificial Intelligence (AI), a game-changer that holds the promise of transforming the way we approach Search Engine Optimization (SEO). At the forefront of this AI revolution is ChatGPT, a marvel of natural language processing that empowers digital marketers with an array of possibilities, particularly in terms of content adaptability and scalability.

Content Adaptability

In the realm of SEO, crafting high-quality and relevant content is a constant challenge. The shift in search algorithms towards valuing user intent and context has made it imperative to produce content that not only addresses user queries but also provides value. This is where generative AI steps in. ChatGPT, armed with its language understanding capabilities, can assist marketers in creating adaptable content that resonates with diverse audiences.

Multilingual Content: With businesses targeting global markets, language barriers can hinder outreach. Generative AI can effortlessly generate content in multiple languages, ensuring your message transcends linguistic boundaries without compromising quality.

Tone and Style Variability: Different audiences demand different tones and styles of communication. Whether It is formal for corporate clients or informal for younger demographics, AI can tailor content to match the desired tone, enhancing engagement and relatability.

Rapid Topic Expansion: Exploring new niches or expanding into adjacent industries can be resource-intensive. Generative AI can expedite content creation by providing well-researched articles, allowing you to diversify your content strategy without excessive time investment.

Scalability

The demand for fresh and engaging content is insatiable, but manual content creation can be a bottleneck. This is where generative AI excels, offering an avenue for seamless scalability.

Bulk Content Generation: Whether It is generating product descriptions for an e-commerce site or creating blog posts for a content-driven strategy, AI can churn out a high volume of content efficiently, freeing up human resources for strategic planning and analysis.

Consistent Brand Voice: Maintaining a consistent brand voice across a multitude of content pieces is challenging. AI-powered tools can ensure your brand's voice remains intact even when generating large volumes of content, bolstering brand identity.

Dynamic SEO Adaptation: Search algorithms are ever-evolving, and so are SEO strategies. Generative AI can swiftly adapt to SEO trends, seamlessly integrating optimized keywords and phrases into generated content to enhance search visibility.

However, It is important to tread cautiously. While generative AI offers remarkable adaptability and scalability, maintaining authenticity and avoiding content that feels robotic is crucial. Striking the right balance between AI-generated content and human touch is key to retaining a genuine connection with your audience.

As the realms of SEO and generative AI converge, the power to adapt content to diverse contexts and scale operations like never before becomes a reality. Embracing this synergy can empower digital marketers to focus on strategic vision while AI handles the heavy lifting of content creation. In the chapters ahead, we will delve deeper into the mechanics of AI-driven content generation and explore strategies to seamlessly incorporate AI into your SEO toolkit.

RISKS OF LATER PENALIZATION

In the quest for efficiency and innovation, leveraging AI-generated content in SEO strategies has become an enticing proposition. Yet, with great power comes the potential for unintended consequences. One significant concern that arises when utilizing AI-generated content is the risk of future penalization from search engines like Google, especially when the content fails to provide genuine value and can be detected as AI-generated.

1. Quality and Relevance: Google's primary goal is to deliver the most relevant and high-quality content to its users. If AI-generated content lacks substance, coherence, and relevance, it could lead to a diminished user experience. Google's algorithms have grown more adept at discerning content quality, and if your AI-generated content fails to meet user expectations, it could result in reduced rankings or even penalties.

2. Duplicated or Plagiarized Content: AI-generated content might inadvertently produce text that resembles existing content on the web. If Google detects significant overlap or outright plagiarism, your website could face penalties for duplicative content. It is crucial to ensure that AI-generated content is original and does not replicate existing material.

3. Unnatural Language and Tone: One of the challenges with AI-generated content is maintaining a natural language flow and tone. If content sounds robotic, overly technical, or deviates from the expected style, Google might consider it spammy or low-quality. Striking a balance between AI assistance and maintaining human-like language is essential.

4. User Engagement Metrics: Google pays close attention to user engagement metrics like bounce rate, time on page, and click-through rate. If AI-generated content fails to engage users and encourages quick exits from your page, it could signal to Google that your content is not meeting user needs, potentially leading to lower rankings.

5. Detection of AI-Generated Content: AI is getting more sophisticated, but search engines are also advancing in their ability to identify AI-generated content. If Google can confidently identify that your content is machine-generated, and it does not meet quality standards, your website could face penalties for attempting to manipulate search rankings.

MITIGATION STRATEGIES

Content Review and Editing: While AI can expedite content creation, human review and editing remain imperative. Ensuring that AI-generated content aligns with your brand voice, is factually accurate, and provides genuine value can mitigate risks.

Value-Centric Approach: Focus on creating content that genuinely answers user queries, offers insights, and adds value. User satisfaction remains a cornerstone of SEO success.

Originality and Attribution: If AI is used to assist in content creation, attribute the content appropriately. Originality and proper sourcing can help demonstrate your commitment to providing authentic value.

Natural Language Mastery: Invest in AI tools that excel in generating natural-sounding language. This can minimize the risk of content sounding automated or overly technical.

Testing and Optimization: Continuously monitor user engagement metrics and gather feedback. Adjust your AI-generated content strategy based on performance data to align with user preferences.

Balancing the benefits of AI-generated content with the risks of Google penalties requires a strategic and cautious approach. The goal is to utilize AI as a tool to enhance content creation rather than replace the creative human touch. By adhering to quality, relevance, and user satisfaction, digital marketers can harness the power of AI while sidestepping potential pitfalls.

THERE IS NO CHOICE TO USE IT

In the dynamic world of digital marketing, staying ahead of the competition is not just a goal; It is a necessity for survival. As technologies continue to evolve, gaining a competitive edge becomes a strategic imperative. The rise of Artificial Intelligence (AI) in content generation has introduced a new paradigm, where the adoption of AI by one player in the market can trigger a chain reaction, compelling others to follow suit to match the advantage gained.

Imagine a scenario where one of your competitors embraces AI-powered content generation to streamline their marketing efforts. The implications of this strategic move can set off a domino effect that reverberates across the industry. Here is how it unfolds:

1. Enhanced Efficiency: AI-generated content can dramatically speed up content creation processes. Your AI-adopting competitor gains the ability to churn out high-quality articles, blog posts, and product descriptions at an unprecedented pace. This agility enables them to be more responsive to market trends and consumer demands.

2. Increased Content Volume: With the ability to produce content at a faster rate, your competitor's online presence expands rapidly. They can cover a wider range of topics, capture long-tail keywords, and address a broader spectrum of user queries.

3. SEO Dominance: A larger volume of content translates to a broader digital footprint, potentially bolstering your competitor's search engine rankings. They might capture more organic traffic, outrank you on key terms, and gain visibility on a scale previously unattainable.

**4. Resource Allocation: By freeing up human resources from manual content creation, your competitor can allocate their creative workforce towards more strategic endeavors, such as campaign planning, data analysis, and customer engagement.

5. Competitive Advantage: As your AI-adopting competitor enjoys the benefits of increased efficiency, enhanced content volume, and improved SEO, they gain a noticeable competitive advantage. Their brand becomes associated with thought leadership, timely responses, and a wealth of informative content.

In the fast-paced world of business, standing still often equates to falling behind. When one competitor reaps the rewards of AI-driven content generation, the pressure mounts on other players to level the playing field. The strategic advantage gained by early AI adopters becomes a motivating force for others to embrace AI to remain competitive.

As AI adoption becomes a market norm, It is not enough to merely implement AI for the sake of keeping up. Careful consideration and strategic planning are essential:

1. Quality Over Quantity: While speed and volume matter, maintaining content quality and authenticity is paramount. AI-generated content must align with your brand voice and provide genuine value to users.

2. Differentiation Through Strategy: Utilize AI-generated content as a tool to bolster your overall content strategy. By incorporating human expertise, unique insights, and creativity, you can stand out in a sea of automated content.

3. Ethical Considerations: Be transparent with your audience about AI involvement in content creation. Honesty and authenticity build trust, which is crucial for long-term success.

4. Continuous Improvement: Regularly analyze the performance of AI-generated content. Gather user feedback, monitor engagement metrics, and refine your approach to align with audience preferences.

In the age of AI, where one competitor's advantage triggers a cascading effect, strategic foresight is paramount. Embracing AI-driven content generation is not just about keeping pace; It is about seizing opportunities, innovating, and maintaining a resilient foothold in an ever-evolving landscape. As the AI revolution reshapes the rules of engagement, It is adapt or be left behind—a rallying cry for digital marketers seeking to thrive in this transformative era.

THE RAND FISHKIN LEAK:

GOOGLE EXPOSED

EXPLAINING THE LEAK

In an unprecedented event, a massive leak of internal Google documents has offered a rare glimpse into the intricate workings of Google's ranking algorithm. The revelations, analyzed by industry experts Rand Fishkin and Michael King, shed light on the multifaceted factors that influence search rankings. This article delves into the key findings from the leaked documents, providing an authoritative yet approachable guide for digital architects and SEO professionals navigating the complex landscape of Google Search.

On March 13, an automated bot named yoshi-code-bot released thousands of documents from Google's internal Content API Warehouse on GitHub. This leak, shared with Rand Fishkin, co-founder of SparkToro, and Michael King, CEO of iPullRank, reveals crucial elements that Google uses to rank content. The implications of this leak are monumental, potentially reshaping our understanding of SEO strategies and Google's search algorithm.

A collection of 2,500 leaked internal documents from Google, filled with details about the data the company collects, has been confirmed as authentic by Google. Until now, Google had refused to comment on the materials.

The documents detail the data that Google is tracking, some of which may be used in its closely guarded search ranking algorithm. They offer an unprecedented — though still murky — look under the hood of one of the most consequential systems shaping the web.

The leaked material suggests that Google collects and potentially uses data that company representatives have previously said does not contribute to ranking webpages in Google Search, such as clicks and Chrome user data. The thousands of pages of documents serve as a repository of information for Google employees, but it's unclear which pieces of data are actually used to rank search content. The information could be outdated, used strictly for training purposes, or collected but not used specifically for Search. The documents also do not reveal how different elements are weighted in search, if at all.

Still, the information made public is likely to cause ripples across the search engine optimization (SEO), marketing, and publishing industries. Google is typically highly secretive about how its search algorithm works, but these documents — along with recent testimony in the US Department of Justice antitrust case — have provided more clarity around what signals Google considers when ranking websites.

THE ESSENTIAL TAKEAWAYS

I won't delve too deeply into the individual ranking factors in the document since there are many. However, here are some particularly interesting and important points for bloggers:

Small Personal Sites/Blogs Attribute: There's an attribute that specifically marks small personal sites and blogs, though its purpose is unclear.

SiteAuthority Score: Google has a siteAuthority score.

NavBoost: This is largely made up of click data, such as the longest click from the SERPs (the search result the user spent the longest time on) and the last good click (the last time someone went to your site and stayed). It tracks clicks over 13 months.

Chrome Visits Tracking: Google tracks Chrome visits across the web to determine user behavior.

Twiddlers: These are re-ranking algorithms that run between major updates and shift rankings in the SERPs.

Over-Optimized Anchor Text: Using over-optimized anchor text, especially consistently for links from third parties, seems to trigger a spam demotion for those links.

Poor Navigation and Exact Match Domains: Both can lower your rankings.

Stored Page Versions: Google stores at least the last 20 versions of your web pages. To have a "clean slate," you probably need to update it more than 20 times. It's unclear how significant a change needs to be to count as a new version.

Font Size and Text Weight: Google tracks these attributes. Larger links seem more positive, and Google reads bolded text differently than normal text, which also improves accessibility.

Keyword Stuffing Score: Google has a keyword stuffing score.

Domain Expiry Tracking: Google tracks when domains expire, so they either already can or soon will be able to detect expired domain abuse.

Video Site Classification: If a site has videos on more than 50% of its pages, it becomes classified as a video site. It's unclear if these videos need to be indexed, be in a certain area of the post, or need to be natively uploaded to the website.

YMYL Content Score: YMYL (Your Money or Your Life) content has its own ranking score.

Gold Standard Attribute: There's a "gold standard" attribute that seems to mark human-generated content, but it's unclear how it's triggered.

AI Overviews: AI Overviews are not mentioned in the document.

Internal Links: There is no clear mention of internal links as an attribute.

Whitelisted Topics: Three topics have "whitelists" (they need to be approved to be shared). These are travel, COVID, and politics. It's unclear if travel sites are for the general SERPs, Google's "travel" section, or even the widgets they pull. Travel being the only non-YMYL niche covered here may be a leftover from the COVID lockdowns and could be defunct.

MEANWHILE IN GOOGLE HQS...

The search community is still digesting the significant reveal of Google Search ranking documents made public. Everyone has been wondering why Google hasn't commented on the leak. Well, Google has finally spoken – we talked to a Google spokesperson about the data leak.

Google informed us that many assumptions being made based on the data leak are out of context, incomplete, and that search ranking signals are constantly evolving. They emphasized that while Google's core ranking principles remain unchanged, the specific and individual signals contributing to Google rankings do change.

A Google spokesperson provided us with the following statement:

"We would caution against making inaccurate assumptions about Search based on out-of-context, outdated, or incomplete information. We've shared extensive information about how Search works and the types of factors that our systems weigh, while also working to protect the integrity of our results from manipulation."

However, Google will not comment on the specifics – which elements are accurate, which are not, which are currently in use, and how strongly they are weighted. Google stated that disclosing such details could enable spammers and bad actors to manipulate the rankings.

Google also noted that it would be incorrect to assume that this data leak is comprehensive, fully relevant, or even provides up-to-date information on its Search rankings.

Did Google lie to us? It's hard to say for certain. Some ranking signals that Google historically claimed not to use were specifically mentioned in the leaked documents. Google's statement implies that information in the documents might never have been used, might have been tested temporarily, or might have changed over the years. Again, Google won't delve into specifics.

Many in the SEO community have long suspected that Google has not been fully transparent and believe in conducting their own testing to determine what works in SEO.

Personally, I tend to trust people who look me in the eye and tell me something. I don't believe the Google representatives I've spoken to over the years lied outright to me. It might be a matter of semantics, the timing of using a specific signal, or perhaps I am just very naive (which is possible) and Google has lied.

Regarding communication, Google assured me they are still committed to providing accurate information but will not provide specific details on a ranking signal-by-signal basis. Google also mentioned that its ranking systems change over time and they will continue to communicate what they can to the community.

Does it matter? Ultimately, all signals point to the same conclusion. Mike King, who was the first to delve into this document and help reveal the details, said that we need to build content and websites that people want to visit, spend time on, click over to, and link to. The best approach is to create a website and content that people enjoy. The role of an SEO is to continue building great sites with great content. It may be a boring answer, but it's the truth.

What happened? As we reported, thousands of documents, seemingly from Google's internal Content API Warehouse, were released on March 13 on GitHub by an automated bot called yoshi-code-bot. These documents were shared with Rand Fishkin, SparkToro co-founder, earlier this month.

Why we care? We've been given a glimpse into how Google's ranking algorithm might work, which is invaluable for SEOs who can decipher its meaning. In 2023, we had an unprecedented look at Yandex Search ranking factors via a leak, which was a major story of that year. This Google leak could be the story of the year – perhaps even the century.

But what should we do with this information? Probably the same thing we've been doing all along – build awesome sites with awesome content.

LATEST SEARCH TRENDS

NEW TREND, NEW HYPE, NEW DISAPPOINTMENT

Recently, innovative search methods have emerged, such as 'circle search,' where users can draw a circle on their smartphone screen to search for the content (image or text) within that circle. Additionally, new developments in video search are on the horizon, complementing existing advancements in image search and augmented reality (AR) search. These technologies promise enhanced user experiences and more intuitive interactions with digital content.

Circle search introduces a novel way to interact with search engines. By simply drawing a circle around an area of interest on their smartphone screens, users can instantly search for information related to that specific segment of an image or text. This method leverages the touchscreen capabilities of modern devices to provide a more tactile and precise search experience. Imagine snapping a photo of a street market and circling a particular fruit stand to find out more about the fruits on display, or highlighting a section of a dense article to pull up related information.

Video search technology is also undergoing significant advancements. Unlike traditional text or image search, video search allows users to find specific moments within videos based on content, context, and even spoken words. This development is particularly exciting as it opens up new possibilities for navigating large volumes of video content efficiently. For example, a user could search for a specific scene in a movie or a particular segment of a lecture without manually scrolling through the entire video.

Despite the potential these technologies hold, widespread adoption remains a significant hurdle. Changing human behavior and search habits is notoriously difficult. While these new search methods offer clear advantages, users are often slow to integrate new behaviors into their daily routines.

Take voice search, for instance. Despite being available and improving in accuracy and convenience over the past several years, it has not yet become the dominant mode of search. Many people still prefer traditional text-based searches due to familiarity and reliability. Voice search adoption has been gradual, and it serves as a pertinent example of the challenges new search technologies face.

GOOGLE POWERED BY REDDIT

In a strategic move to strengthen its Search business, Google has recently expanded its partnership with Reddit. This collaboration will enhance Google users' access to the wealth of authentic, human conversations and experiences on Reddit, making it easier to find valuable information.

This long-term collaboration will deepen, with Reddit playing a significant role on the open internet. A key component of this partnership is a new Cloud collaboration, allowing Reddit to integrate AI-powered capabilities using Vertex AI. Reddit plans to utilize Vertex AI to improve search functionalities and other features on its platform.

The initiative responds to the growing trend of users searching Google for content on Reddit, such as product recommendations and travel advice. Additionally, Google will gain access to Reddit's Data API, which provides real-time, structured, and unique content from Reddit's extensive platform.

This access allows Google to efficiently obtain fresher information and enhanced signals to better understand Reddit content. Google can use this data to display, train on, and otherwise leverage Reddit information accurately and relevantly.

The partnership does not alter Google's use of publicly available, crawlable content for indexing, training, or display in its products. Instead, it supports more content-forward displays of Reddit information, making Google products more helpful and facilitating user participation in Reddit communities.

Valued at $60 million annually for Reddit, the deal grants Google exclusive access to Reddit's data for use in Search and its generative AI projects. This structured access to a broader range of Reddit content will improve language models' ability to understand human conversations and writing styles, influencing content understanding and ranking in Google Search.

However, the partnership also highlights potential overlaps and conflicts in content moderation policies. For instance, if a company like Techify becomes the target of negative discussions on Reddit, its reputation could suffer. Reddit's emphasis on free expression and community-driven moderation might clash with Google's stricter content guidelines, raising questions about balancing user safety standards with Reddit's approach to content.

As Reddit content becomes more prevalent in search results, brands may find themselves exposed to unfiltered discussions on the platform, impacting their online reputation. This scenario underscores the need for a nuanced approach to content moderation, requiring collaboration between brands, platform operators, and search engine providers to maintain open discourse while protecting users from harmful content.

Navigating the intersection of Reddit and Google's content moderation policies will be crucial as platform boundaries blur, ensuring a positive online presence and fostering a safe, open online environment.

Google's new artificial intelligence (AI) search feature is under fire for delivering erratic and inaccurate responses.

The experimental "AI Overviews" tool has provided some bizarre advice, such as suggesting the use of "non-toxic glue" to make cheese stick to pizza and recommending that geologists advise eating one rock per day. These answers, seemingly sourced from Reddit comments or satirical articles from The Onion, have been widely mocked on social media.

A Google spokesperson told the BBC that these were "isolated examples" and insisted that the feature generally performs well. "The examples we've seen are generally very uncommon queries and aren't representative of most people's experiences," they stated. "The vast majority of AI overviews provide high-quality information, with links to dig deeper on the web." Google also noted that they have addressed "policy violations" and are using the feedback to improve their systems.

This isn't Google's first issue with AI-powered products. In February, the company paused its chatbot Gemini due to criticism over its "woke" responses. Its predecessor, Bard, also had a rocky start.

Google began testing AI overviews in search results for a small group of logged-in UK users in April and expanded the feature to all US users in mid-May during its annual developer showcase. The tool uses AI to summarize search results, saving users from scrolling through lengthy lists of websites. Although experimental, it is expected to see widespread use given Google's dominance in the search market, with over 90% of global market share according to Statcounter.

The AI-driven search approach is seen by many industry experts as the future, despite concerns about the environmental impact of power-hungry technology. The concept is appealing—why sift through pages of results and ads when a chatbot can provide a single, definitive answer? However, this only works if the answers are trustworthy.

Generative AI "hallucinations" are a problem not just for Google but for other tech companies as well. For instance, a reporter searching whether gasoline could cook spaghetti faster received the response: "no... but you can use gasoline to make a spicy spaghetti dish," complete with a recipe.

While the number of correct searches isn't as widely shared on social media, it is clear that AI search must handle all types of queries, including unusual ones. Rival firms also face backlash for integrating more AI tools into consumer products. The UK's data watchdog is investigating Microsoft for a new feature that takes continuous screenshots of online activity on its AI-focused PCs. Additionally, OpenAI faced criticism from actress Scarlett Johansson for using a voice similar to hers after she declined their request to voice their chatbot.

Despite these challenges, Google's AI search remains crucial to its business model, and the company is keen to protect and future-proof this service.

PART I
SEO

FIRST:

PUTTING IN PLACE A SEARCH STRATEGY

Search Engine Optimization, or SEO, is the subset of search engine marketing that focuses on improving your visibility in organic or unpaid search results. It applies both to your regular website content and to your e-commerce product listings, and it impacts results shown across both desktop and mobile devices.

Despite advances in other digital marketing channels, organic search remains one of the most popular ways for visitors to discover you - 3.5 billion searches are performed worldwide on Google every day! Organic results are typically responsible for up to half of all website traffic, and a large majority of searchers still favor organic search results over paid listings, which they deem less reliable in terms of quality and credibility.

In this book, we will explore exactly what organic search is and how it works, the key elements that go into creating an effective SEO strategy, and how best to go about achieving your desired SEO outcomes.

SETTING A SEO STRATEGY

In order to optimize your site content for organic search, It is important to first understand how search results are generated.

The journey from a user's search query to the generated search results page, or SERP, starts with the search engine's index. This is a huge database of information on billions of websites, which is used to evaluate the relevance of webpages to search queries.

To build this index, search engines use automated bots - often referred to as "crawlers"

- which search through pages of websites, looking for clues about the subject of each one in everything from the text, titles, headers, keywords, and images; to other information such as 'inbound links' and social signals. They also assess how fast each page loads, and follow the links included on the page to access other areas within the site. And these bots work fast, typically crawling thousands of pages every second.

When the user enters the search query, the search engine's complex proprietary algorithms then determine from this index which pages will appear on the results page, as well as the order of display.

The workings of the algorithms themselves are closely guarded secrets. Some elements are known or are at least obvious, and SEO tactics are designed to take maximum advantage of them. In general, the most important factors to your site being well- regarded by search engines are mobile responsiveness, speed of loading, and above all, good and valuable content. However, algorithms are amended almost every day, sometimes in major ways. It can be quite an undertaking for SEO practitioners to keep up, and sites can sometimes drop down or even out of search results without warning.

The competition to appear on the first page of the results can be intense. In an effort to make search results more intuitive – and to provide searchers with the answers they need without having to click through to any other site – results pages will often include elements other than organic results alone. This might include carousels, videos, images, knowledge boxes, or even paid ads. Accordingly, for some searches only eight or nine organic links are now typically displayed on Google's results page, as opposed to the previous standard of 10.

Results pages are also becoming much more personalized, often taking into account elements such as location, browser, and search history, or even any linked online accounts. Search engines are aiming to provide the best results for each specific user, and this means that for different people, the same search may pull different results. For instance, it can be very misleading to look up your company on your own browser!

When it comes to forming your SEO strategy, as with any digital marketing channel, the right place to start is defining clear goals and measures of success.

When choosing SEO goals, It is important to keep in mind your wider business strategy. Rather than just monitoring where you appear in search engine rankings for various search phrases, you should look for the rankings and the keywords - by which we mean the words or phrases you are looking to rank for - that generate the most qualified traffic, leads and conversions, and work to optimize and leverage those to maximum effect. If your SEO campaign increases search impressions and visitor numbers but you see no impact on business outcomes, then It is likely that you are optimizing for the wrong keywords, or attracting the wrong visitors entirely.

SEO can be employed to help support a variety of business objectives:

Take increasing brand awareness. Here, the aim is getting your company to appear in search results frequently. In order to give the impression that you are a credible authority in your industry or marketplace, this should cover both branded keywords (those that include your company name) and non-branded keywords. This is all about brand recognition and not specifically sales, so you need to think about how you want to communicate your uniqueness, expertise, and values. For example, a gardening supplies company might target keywords such as "growing roses" or "landscaping ideas."

You might want to focus on increasing traffic. This may sound like a fairly obvious goal, but by this, we mean increasing qualified traffic. Increasing visitors who will never be prospects for your business is a wasted effort, so your SEO goal in this regard should be focused on attracting actual customers.

Perhaps you want to promote your products or services. It can be difficult to correlate exactly how many conversions can be attributed to each digital marketing channel. However, since we know that prospects do use search during their decision-making process, it would be reasonable to expect that improving organic search visibility for specific products should contribute to increased sales and revenue.

In addition to highlighting products or services, you may also want to improve your rank for specific keywords or with specific pages, thus promoting your expertise and the content of those pages.

Whatever your desired outcomes, the SEO goals that you set should be doable, understandable, measurable, and beneficial – or DUMB.

By Doable, we mean your goals should be realistic and achievable. For example, if the current top-ranking positions for your important keywords are taken by companies with more resources and an established track record in terms of optimization, site authority and backlinks; then perhaps you should consider scaling back your expectations, or prioritizing fewer outcomes.

Your goals also need to be Understandable: everyone involved in your SEO campaigns should be able to articulate them.

For a goal to be helpful, it should be Measurable – specifically, you need to be able to track your progress towards achieving it. As such, It is important to develop SEO-related KPIs and associated metrics.

And finally, as mentioned, your SEO goals should be Beneficial to your business by supporting your wider business goals.

When it comes to tracking your progress towards your chosen SEO goals, there are many possible KPIs you can use. Again, It is important to focus on improving specific areas and supporting your business goals, so It is best to work with only a few KPIs at a time. It is rarely helpful to simply produce a rankings or traffic report without further qualification as to whether the visitors clicked-through from results pages, or whether the visitors were qualified and converted at a reasonable rate.

Let us consider the potential SEO goals we discussed earlier, and think about how we might track them.

Increasing brand awareness: improvements in brand awareness should lead to an increase in branded searches, as well as mentions of your brand on social media and other postings. These can be tracked using news alerts, a reputation monitoring service, or various types of branding studies.

Increasing traffic: your analytics reports should show you numbers of visitors from organic search and allow you to segment these further by criteria such as country, time on site, or conversions. This allows you to measure KPIs that go beyond the raw number of visitors to look at traffic quality, such as "number of conversions from organic search," or "increase in page views per session from organic search."

If you are working on increasing the number of links to your site, then your referral traffic – that is, the visitors from links on other sites - should also increase. In the same way, you can measure the sheer numbers, or you can go deeper and look at the quality of these visitors.

Promoting your products or services. In addition to tracking conversions for the specific products or services you were looking to promote, you might want to look at KPIs such as "number of organic search impressions," "average search position" or "organic click- through rate"

And finally, rankings for specific keywords. Here, you might want to review KPIs such as "percentage of keywords in top 20 positions", or "share of search" – the percentage of times that your site appeared in results pages for a given keyword. To track KPIs like this, a number of tools are available which provide lists of your average keyword rankings, with some even providing competitor results and analysis.

Whilst It is possible to see the number of visitors from organic search to any given page, Google no longer provides analytics tools with information that relates specific keywords to specific landing pages or user actions. However, if you know what the topic and content of that landing page are, you should have some idea of what the keywords might have been.

Due to the ongoing and unpredictable nature of SEO (particularly in comparison with the immediacy of paid search), it can be difficult to estimate timelines or desired return on investment, especially at the beginning of an SEO campaign. The most important overall outcomes from your SEO efforts should be increased quality traffic, visitor engagement, backlinks, and conversions. Take careful benchmarks of these metrics at the outset, and review them regularly so that you can learn what is and is not working, and make the appropriate adjustments to your tactics and resources as you progress.

PUTTING IT INTO PLACE

Once you have your goals and KPIs in place for your SEO efforts, It is time to start thinking about how you can go about achieving them.

One of the most important aspects of search engine marketing in general is selecting the most appropriate keywords on which to focus. The whole premise of search is that visitors are looking for something, and your keywords will control whether your site is a contender to be shown to them.

Before we dive into specific tactics and techniques for performing keyword research, there are a few concepts we should clear up.

Within search, a search query or search term is the actual word or set of words that the user enters into the search engine. It is important to appreciate that these can be slightly different from the keywords you have chosen to compete for, but the search engine's algorithm may decide that they are similar enough for your site to be displayed in the search results. Sometimes these will be common synonyms or misspellings, the same words as your keywords but in a different order, or even closely related searches.

For example, the search query "women's trousers" might trigger search results for sites that are optimized for "women's trousers," but also "ladies' trousers," "women's slacks," "women's wide-leg trousers," and so on. In paid search, you can exclude any of the keywords that you do not want to appear for, but in SEO there is not much you can do other than to reconsider your keywords.

Branded keywords are those that include the name of your business or organization. Whilst branded searches can indicate awareness of your company within your target audience, there is likely little you need to do about branded keywords from an SEO perspective. If you have an existing website for your business, it should always appear at the top of search results for your business.

However, by definition, only people who have already heard of you can do branded searches. Everyone else has to find you by looking for what you do rather than who you are; so, It is vital to develop and optimize for non-branded or "generic" keywords to attract new visitors.

Beyond branded and non-branded, keywords can also be categorized into "short-tail" and "long-tail." Short-tail searches are those that comprise only one or two keywords, such as "hiking boots." Search queries with more words are known as "long-tail," because the frequency of searches for each one is much lower, but there are essentially unlimited possibilities for word combinations. In fact, 15% of Google searches every day have never been made! Long-tail keywords are usually created by adding modifiers to the central keyword, such as the location ("buy hiking boots in London") or other specifics ("waterproof hiking boots").

Since there tends to be much less competition for long-tail keywords, they are much easier to optimize and rank for. If you only focus on short-tail keywords, you may be missing a lot of opportunities. Whilst there are fewer searches for more detailed phrases, each additional word gives you more specific detail that can be used to take the visitor to the most relevant pages on your site, and the visitors who use them are far more likely to convert as they have already clarified their exact needs.

One of the most important aspects of keyword research and selection is understanding user intent. Here, you need to develop an understanding of where visitors are in the customer journey – that is, the different stages that customers typically go through when deciding to do business with you. The "intent" behind the search will largely govern whether a landing page will meet the visitor's needs, or whether they will bounce quickly – which is not helpful to them, or to your SEO efforts.

When entering a search query, the mindset of visitors can broadly be broken down into four categories:

In the case of a navigational search, the user already knows what they are looking for. Typically, this includes branded keywords, specific names of companies, products, or services, or known URLs that the user puts into the search box. Since they are essentially branded searches, you do not need to do much to optimize for them.

The most common type of searches are informational. Here, users are looking for answers to questions or researching products and services, usually without any immediate intention to buy. This could be questions for which there is a short and non- controversial factual answer ("When was Marie Curie's birthday?"); or questions that might require longer answers for which there might be alternatives ("Which is the best Thai restaurant near me?"). Within the customer journey, these types of searches are usually at the consideration stage, in which the customer is deciding whether or not to do business with you.

Transactional searches are done in the later stages of the customer journey, at which point the user is ready to convert. These often take the form of very specific, long-tail queries like part numbers for equipment, or flight dates and airports; or could include words such as "buy," "discount," or "sign up."

And finally, around a quarter of searches are considered ambiguous. Although the different types of searches are relatively straightforward to describe, in reality It is often difficult to determine the user intent simply from looking at the search query itself. For example, a search for "bicycle chain repair" might suggest that the searcher wants to find a shop to fix a bike or buy a part - both transactional searches, or they might want to find a video on bike repair: an informational search.

Wherever possible, assign a user intent to each keyword, and tailor the landing page you are optimizing for each to the appropriate visitor mindset. It can be easy to fall into the trap of assuming – or hoping – that every search is transactional, and treating every visitor as if they are a potential customer looking to buy immediately. Unfortunately, It is rarely the case - fewer than 10% of searches are transactional - and it can be very counterproductive to direct visitors who are actually doing research to a landing page that screams "buy now" but fails to provide any helpful information.

When it comes to actually finding the best keywords for you, the place to start is developing an initial keyword list upon which to build. Begin by thinking in broad terms about what searchers might be looking for. There is no hard and fast rule about the length of this list, and of course it depends on the size of your site, but It is good practice to start with a lot of keywords that are grouped in line with the content areas of your site, and to then filter and prioritize.

Overall, you are looking for the words that your target markets might use to describe your products and services at various stages of their customer journey. There are many tools available to help you with this: by entering some typical search terms that you are interested in, these tools will show you the monthly search volume, the current level of competition, and offer alternative keyword suggestions. More in-depth tools will even provide information about how your competitors are ranking for the keywords you are looking at, which can be particularly helpful for gauging the relative value of those keywords, and the level of competition to rank for them.

If you are already running a paid search campaign, monitoring your best performing keywords in terms of conversions and click-throughs can also provide you with some insight into the most valuable keywords or types of keywords for your business.

To keep track of your research, it can be helpful to create a keyword research spreadsheet. Whether you use a template or design your own, for each keyword or phrase you cover you should include, at a minimum: the keyword, its content or topic grouping, the associated user intent, whether It is short or long-tail, the search volume, the level of competition, the keyword value, and the priority you assign it.

Once you have your preliminary list of keywords, do some searches for them - preferably using an anonymous browser to avoid the results being personalized to you - and look at the results pages that currently appear. What types of content come up - videos, images, blog posts, product listings? And importantly, are there any gaps in the information that you could fill?

To filter and prioritize your list, look for the optimal combination of higher levels of value and search volumes combined with lower levels of competition and difficulty. Consider how best you can support your defined goals and how quickly you can create the required content; and prioritize your list accordingly. But remember: this list is just a starting point, and should be added to and refined as you learn from your SEO efforts.

Beyond selecting and refining your keywords, you will also need to decide who will put your SEO strategy into action. A question that is often asked is whether you should perform SEO in-house, or whether you should hire an agency to help you. Of course, the answer is dependent on considerations such as your own budget and resources, your current skillset, and the amount of time you could commit to an SEO effort; and bear in mind that even if you do outsource much of the work, successful SEO requires the creation of high- quality and valuable content which you will still need to oversee...

But to whom exactly can you outsource?

Reputable agencies can be relatively expensive, but come with a depth of expertise, access to a wide variety of paid tools, familiarity with the latest algorithm changes, and a wide body of knowledge gathered through experimenting and testing different SEO techniques across a range of customers. However, if you do hire an agency, you should still ensure that you have some basic SEO knowledge in-house so that you can understand the tactics that are being suggested, as well as the results that are being reported and how well their performance is meeting your expectation.

On the other hand, you may choose to work with consultants. Those with the relevant expertise can advise you on strategy and tactics, and can guide your team through implementing these.

No matter who you work with, you should ask them about their approach to keyword research and usage, page optimization, and link building; check their references; and always be wary of anyone who says they can "guarantee results" - often, this is a red flag that they might resort to using "black hat SEO" tactics in order to show you short-term success.

Given that SEO is a long-term and unpredictable discipline that requires sustained monitoring and effort, It is not entirely surprising that some have attempted to find and exploit shortcuts... and indeed, still do today. These techniques, which breach search engine guidelines, are referred to under the term 'black hat SEO.'

Some are fairly rudimentary such as keyword stuffing, the practice of filling a page with keywords that are irrelevant, or repeating keywords so often that the content is difficult to read, in order to rank for keywords that your content does not actually reflect. Some 'crafty' black hat practitioners even hide keywords by including them in the same color as the page background so they appear to web crawlers, but not to visitors.

Another technique is known as cloaking, where potentially thousands of pages of content are created, but not for the benefit of human visitors... instead, they are shown only to the search engine with the intention of manipulating the algorithm. Here, the server distinguishes between actual human visitors and crawlers. It then produces a different version of the page for each, with the aim of deceiving the search engine into indexing for keywords or content which are not reflected on the actual page – that is, the one shown to users.

There are many other techniques like this, however, these tactics are not without consequence. Regardless of the level of sophistication, search engines, over time, have become extremely adept at detecting this kind of behavior. In fact, if used, they can ultimately lead to your site being penalized or even removed from appearing in search results. Ultimately, if you are engaging in activity that search engines have outlined as unacceptable, then you are not doing SEO, what you are doing is referred to as 'web spam.' Those who take this risk knowingly are generally not worried about the potential penalties, and when it happens, they will simply move on to another disposable website.

However, as an established business with a long-term SEO strategy, these are risks that you just cannot afford to be taking, so It is vital to always know exactly what efforts are being made on your behalf.

It is possible to find sites that are doing well in search which clearly employ these tactics. For this reason, some people believe that It is worth trying "black hat" SEO, at least for short-term gain. In the long run however, It is very likely that the offending site will be detected and penalized, and once these punishments are imposed, it can be very difficult to have them reversed.

ON SITE SEO

All good SEO activity starts with planning your strategy and selecting the right keywords for your site. But once that is done, how do you actually go about optimizing your site so that search engines understand what you are offering and display you on the results page for the most relevant queries?

This is what is known as 'on-site SEO,' because it involves the actions you take on your site, as opposed to elsewhere on the web, to boost your site's positioning within search engine results pages, also known as your search ranking. There are three main areas of your site that need optimizing for search: the site structure, the source code, and the body copy.

WEBSITE STRUCTURE

When you hear people talking about the 'structure,' 'architecture' or 'hierarchy' of a website, it just refers to how the site is organized – in other words, how different pages on the site link to one another. A well-structured site is important for both visitors and search engines. Visitors want to find what they need quickly and easily, while search engines use the structure to understand what the site is about and the relationships between different areas of content.

When it comes to designing the hierarchy of your site, you essentially have two choices: a deep hierarchy and a flat hierarchy. Deep hierarchies look more vertical when they are mapped out: you start with few headings, each linking to a small number of sub-headings, which in turn each link to another small set of sub-levels, and so on.

A flat hierarchy looks more horizontal – you start off with more headings, and the rest of your site's content is listed under one of these.

The hierarchy that works best for your site will depend on your content. However, the flat hierarchy is often recommended as the best approach from an SEO perspective, simply because it reduces the number of 'clicks' that search crawlers need to make to find your content, which is usually recommended to be no more than four.

When deciding on your site hierarchy, it can be very helpful to draw a diagram that maps out all of your main headings, categories, and sub-categories. This allows you to check the flow and logic of your design, and to ensure that all of your content is included.

However, you choose to structure your site, your pages' web addresses - also known as URLs - should reflect that structure, and the keywords you have chosen. If you are aiming for a maximum of four levels, then, rather than using generic headings that do not give any idea of the actual content of the page, structuring the URL as domain/category/sub- category/destination page is a helpful place to start.

Your site hierarchy and URLs will come together to form what is known as a sitemap – essentially a list of all the pages within your website, organized in a logical manner, with categories and headings. There are two types of sitemap: HTML and XML.

An HTML sitemap is an actual page on your website. These kinds of sitemap are very helpful for visitors, especially if the site has a lot of content, but they are not essential for SEO, though they are recommended.

An XML sitemap is a file, intended for use by search engines. It contains, among other things, your page URLs and the date they were last updated, allowing the crawler to check them against the date of its last visit and quickly see which pages need to be checked for updates.

XML sitemaps can be generated automatically using one of the many free tools available online. Any pages that you do not want to be indexed for public search, such as login pages or password protected material, should be excluded from your XML sitemap. Once your file is created, you will need to submit it to each search engine that you want to index your site – and each individual search engine will have instructions available for how to do this.

Beyond the site hierarchy, you will also want to consider your internal links.

Internal links are hyperlinks between pages on your site – a 'related products' link, for example, which leads to other, relevant content on your site. They can be very useful in limiting the number of clicks that visitors need to make, and in helping the search engines to crawl your site. Using links to connect pages with related content, products or services is much more visitor-friendly than trying to convey all of this information through the website menu and navigation tabs.

One particularly helpful form of internal linking is to use breadcrumbs. These are the navigational links you see at the top or bottom of a webpage that show visitors where they are in the site hierarchy and allow them to quickly access previous pages. For SEO purposes, breadcrumbs help search crawlers understand the site structure and will sometimes appear on the search engine results page instead of the page title.

Internal links are not just useful for navigation – they can also improve your page's search ranking through something called link equity, also known as link juice. Search engines will ascribe a certain level of link equity to individual pages on your site, according – among other things – to how recently they were updated, and the quality and relevance of the page with regards to your chosen keywords. Pages with higher link equity can pass 'authority' on to the pages they link to – so if you have a high-ranking page, including internal links to other pages could help you boost those pages' search rankings.

When you are planning out your internal links, look at the common paths that customers take through your website that lead to conversions. What are the key pages – or pieces of content – that you want visitors and search crawlers to find? Make sure your anchor text – the actual words that users click to follow the link – contains your keywords and accurately reflects the topic of the destination page. That way, both visitors and search crawlers know where the link is taking them, and potential customers are more likely to click a descriptive link than one that just says 'click here' or 'learn more'.

If you end up with a broken link – one that does not lead anywhere, or leads to somewhere you did not intend – you need to find it and fix it quickly. Online tools are capable of reporting any missing pages or broken links back to you. If broken links lead to a page that is been deleted or permanently moved, the browser will display a 404 'page not found' error. If this is the case, try including a custom 404 page that contains links to your other, relevant content to allow users and crawlers to find their way back to your site.

One word of warning when it comes to site structure: if the site you want to optimize already exists, be careful about tampering with its current structure. If some of its pages already have excellent search engine positioning, do not rename, or remove them – if you do, you will risk taking away the equity that you have built for those pages, and probably doing more harm than good to your overall search rankings in the process. A better practice is to include a permanent '301 redirect' for the old URL, which basically means that users and search engines are rerouted to the new page, or to the most relevant page if the content has been removed.

You might find there are areas of your website that you do not want to appear in search results, like member-only, password protected pages. In these cases, you need to specifically tell the search crawlers not to include these pages when they crawl your site. To do that, you will need to create a robots.txt file.

Robots.txt is a text file found at 'your site's address.com/robots.txt' that tells search crawlers how to index your site. You can specify your high priority pages to ensure they are indexed, or included in search engines' databases of sites. You can also list URLs of pages on your site that should not be crawled, and provide the locations of your sitemaps so that the crawlers can find them easily and follow all of their links.

It is not compulsory to create a robots.txt file – if search crawlers do not find one for your site, they will crawl your site as normal and assume that every page should be indexed.

It is worth noting that using robots.txt to tell crawlers not to index a certain page will not necessarily prevent them from doing so if they can still get to the page via links from other parts of the site. Also, be aware that the robots.txt file is publicly available, so It is not a good idea to list any pages that you would not want people to know about! In both of these situations, the only way to prevent crawlers indexing these pages is to include a robots meta tag.

A robots meta tag is a piece of code included in the source code of your page – in other words, the 'language' read and used by a browser to display a webpage. It can prevent indexing at an individual page level by using the 'noindex' tag, and tell crawlers not to follow links from the page or create a cached copy of the page - in other words, a temporary saved copy. This can be especially helpful if you need to create duplicate copies of a page – a printer-friendly version, for example – which would diminish the original page's search ranking if crawlers were to find identical content available in multiple places.

However, you choose to structure your site, the main thing to keep in mind is: make it logical. If users can't work out how to navigate to the content they are looking for, they'll leave – and if they can't manage it, search crawlers won't either, and you will end up missing out when it comes to your positioning on the results page.

OPTIMIZING YOUR PAGES

Once you have considered how to optimize your site overall, It is time to think about optimizing individual pages for search.

The page source code is key to this; and among the most significant areas of the source code is the <head> section. This contains information about the page that is not visible in browsers, generally known as metadata.

When it comes to optimizing individual pages, one of the most important areas of the <head> section is the title tag. Make sure you do not confuse it with the meta title tag which is no longer used by search engines, or with the header tag that sits at the top of the page's body copy.

The title tag forms the heading you see on the search results page, or when a link to the page is posted on social media – so rather than opting for something generic like 'About Us' or 'Home Page,' choose a tag that actually tells users about the page and persuades them to follow the link. However, be aware that tags longer than 60 characters risk being cut short on the results page. You do want to include your primary keywords, but do it in a way that seems natural rather than stuffing your title tag full of them.

If you want to include your company name in the title tag, put it at the end rather than at the beginning, because keywords closer to the start of the tag carry greater weight with search engines.

You will need to use a different title tag for every page of your site to avoid any potential issues with duplicate content. If search engines find the same content replicated in different locations, it could suggest that you are copying and pasting rather than creating unique content - and, whether you are copying from your own site or someone else's, It is a red flag to search engines that the contents of your page are not providing any unique value. Occasionally Google rewrites title tags for the results page, which may be a warning that your page has good content, but that your title tag needs work.

The next element of your source code we are going to look at is the meta-description tag. It looks like this:

<meta name="description" content="The text of your meta-tag goes here">

and It is used to provide a brief description of the page. Although it does not directly contribute to search ranking, It is often used by search engines to form the descriptive text below the heading on the results page. This is your chance to write something that really showcases the value for the user of clicking on your link, so make sure it reads naturally, includes keywords, and talks about the benefits of the page content.

Just like your title tags, your meta-description tags need to be unique for every page. If search engines discover duplicate descriptions, or if they determine that your description does not match the page content, you risk triggering spam flags and witnessing a drop in your search rankings.

If Google does detect that something is not right with your meta-descriptions, it might select alternative text from somewhere else on your page. If this happens, try rewriting your meta-descriptions, or testing different versions.

Then there are canonical tags. They look like this:

<link rel="canonical" href=https://example.com/your-primary-page"/>

and they are used when you have multiple URLs pointing to the same content – for example, if you have different versions of a page for different devices – to prevent search engines from penalizing you for having duplicate content.

In this situation, you can specify the primary page to be indexed by including the URL within the canonical tag. If you then include that same canonical tag in the <head> section of the duplicate versions of that page, crawlers will largely ignore them and you should not find your search ranking suffering.

Canonical issues can also be caused by the different ways in which a URL can be written. For example, It is clear to us humans that these refer to the same home page:

domain.com/home www.domain.com

However, to a search crawler these are different URLs, and so could lead to duplicate content issues. Because you cannot control exactly how other sites will write your URL when they link to you – which hopefully they will! - It is good practice to always include a canonical tag on your home page so that crawlers will recognize yours as the original and ignore any other versions of the URL.

Something that can have a positive impact on your SEO rankings, perhaps counterintuitively, are links away from your page to other high-quality sites and content. That is because – providing the other site really is high-quality – outbound links demonstrate that you are credible, that you have relationships in your industry or field, and that you are providing value and additional resources for your visitors.

Any outbound links you do include should be clearly related to the topic of the page. You do not want to fill your pages with outbound links – ideally you should not have more than two or three per page. After all, remember that outbound links do take visitors away from your site, so make sure they open in a new browser tab so that your visitors can easily come back to you when they are ready.

You might also want to include links or buttons to share your content on social media. Different search engines place different value on your content receiving likes and shares on social media, but ultimately your content being shared demonstrates that It is clearly high-quality and valuable, which is exactly what search engines are looking for.

Choose the social platforms that are appropriate for your target audience and content, and make it as easy as possible for users to share your page's content by offering a pre- formatted post that they can simply 'click to share' rather than expecting them to copy, paste and contextualize your URL.

Outside of the individual elements of your page, there are some further technical considerations that will impact the search ranking for pages on your site. One of these is page loading speed. Visitors will quickly leave your page if it takes too long to load; plus, search crawlers will only dedicate a certain amount of time to crawling your site, so if It is wasted while your pages load, they might not get around to indexing the rest of your content.

Another technical consideration you will want to get to grips with is Transport Layer Security, or TLS. You might be more familiar with this under the term Secure Sockets Layer or SSL certificate, which was retired and replaced with TLS.

Have you ever visited a website and spotted that the 'http' at the beginning of the URL has changed to 'https'? That is the indication that the site has TLS – a security protocol that keeps all the data you exchange with that site – credit card numbers or passwords, for example, private and safe from hacking.

Google takes the certification so seriously that It is now included as a factor in how high your site will rank within the results, and their web browser even warns users if they try to visit a site that is not certified.

All this talk of tags, links and technology might seem complicated, but remember that It is just a way of communicating what your site is about, and how to navigate, it to search crawlers. Think of them as signs that tell Google or other search engines that you are credible and trustworthy, and that you deserve that prime placing on the results page.

SEO AND BODY COPY

As well as the way you structure your site and the code that tells the browser what to display when a user loads your website, the body copy of the site itself – in other words, the actual text that a user sees on your page – heavily impacts that page's search rankings.

So how do you create content for your site that will help bolster your search rankings? One method is to use headings.

Headings in the body copy of the page are indicated by header tags. HTML - the standard language used in creating websites - allows for up to six 'levels 'of headings, in descending order of significance, so <h1> is the most important. Any text you put between <h1> tags will generally appear in larger, bold font. <h2> to <h6> tags are useful if you need further headings to break up the text, but they do not carry the same weight when it comes to SEO.

<h1> tags tell both visitors and search engines what the page is about, so you should have unique text for each page. As with title tags, you will be penalized by the search engines if they deem your <h1> text irrelevant to the content of the page, or find you have duplicated the same text elsewhere.

When it comes to the content of the page, your keywords are important, and you should ensure they appear in the first 100-150 words of copy – but do not sacrifice the quality of your content in doing so. Search engines will take engagement metrics such as bounce rate - the number of people who abandon your site without making a second click - and dwell time - how long people spend on your site on average - into account, so creating high-quality, grammatically correct content that is readable and relevant is by far the most important on-site factor in determining your search rankings. And of course, if you are ensuring the content relates to the topic of the page, you should not have to try to include keywords – they should just occur naturally within the text.

Just as you need to guard against duplicating your content across multiple pages, you should also be careful about having multiple pages focused on the same keywords. This can lead to a situation known as 'keyword cannibalization' where your pages end up competing with each other for positions on the results page for that keyword, and you lose control over which one is displayed. So, It is a good idea to limit the focus of each page to just one keyword, and to use variations of that keyword if you have other pages with similar content.

If the text of your page contains information that is naturally structured – for example, a recipe or a list – you might want to use Google's 'Structured

Data Markup Helper' tool. This allows you to indicate each separate element of your list to Google, which basically means that Google is able to better understand your content, and therefore to show it in response to relevant keywords. So, if you have a recipe for muffins that lists blueberries within the ingredients, Google can show your page when users search for 'recipes with blueberries.'

It is not just written copy that search engines take into account either. Incorporating media such as audio, video, infographics, and diagrams on your page can increase visitor engagement and dwell time, but be aware that any images you incorporate could be returned as results on Google's Image Search - so if you are using images there is a whole other results page for you to think about! The good news is, optimizing your images will help your results for both regular and image-based results pages.

Just as you would with URLs, you should use descriptive keywords as the filenames of your images rather than giving them generic labels; so, "pincushion-cactus.jpg" is much more effective than "image1.jpg."

Alternative text tags are used to specify the words to display when an image cannot be shown in the browser - for example, when your internet connection is too slow for images to load. These should describe the image, and also include any relevant keywords.

For example, the alternative text tag for pincushion-cactus.jpg might be 'small flowering pincushion cactus': <img src="pincushion-cactus.jpg" alt="small flowering pincushion cactus"/>.

Essentially, your aim in writing body copy should be to make the message of your content as clear as possible to users and search engines, to offer real value, and to demonstrate why your page is relevant.

Although there are a few technical tips for helping the search engines understand what you are offering, you should not really find yourself having to go too far out of your way to optimize the text that visitors see for search

– as long as your site genuinely provides what you claim it does, there should not be reason to worry.

OFFSITE SEO

Alongside forming a holistic SEO strategy, and optimizing your site and its individual pages for search prominence - a discipline known as 'On Site' SEO - the other arm of your search optimization efforts is known as 'Off Site' SEO.

'Off site SEO' refers to the factors that can impact your site's search ranking but which are external to your site... and therefore less under your direct control. These external factors are considered very important because they demonstrate to search engines that your site is seen by objective third parties as having authority, relevance, and popularity.

In this chapter we will explore what those external factors are, how your efforts can influence them, and how you can go about ensuring that search engines' opinions of how others perceive your site and content match up with all the hard work you put in.

THE IMPORTANCE OF LINKS

There are a variety of 'positive' off site factors including online reviews, social sharing and "liking" of your content which all contribute to your credibility. Search engines can add social media postings to their wider index - although they tend to do this to a limited degree - so links to your site from social platforms can also boost your search visibility.

However, by far the most significant off-site factors are links back to your pages from other quality sites, known as 'backlinks.' High value links are probably the largest single component of search engine algorithms and have been for some time, so they play a major role in your ability to improve your rankings.

So why exactly are links so important?

In the context of SEO, links carry so much weight because they are seen by search engines as an intentional endorsement by another brand, or influencer, of your site or content. There are a few reasons for viewing a link in this way:

First, it takes a conscious effort to place an external link into a website or blog. Unlike social media postings where you can easily click a "share" or "like" button to complete the action, the site owner has to decide where on their page to place the link as well as what the anchor text should say, and then make the corresponding code changes.

Again, unlike a fleeting social media posting or comment which disappears very quickly, It is 'permanent' - a link on a website stays in view whenever the page is displayed.

And above all, It is a major statement. Any 'outbound' link by definition has the potential to take visitors away from the endorsing site. If the site owner is willing to risk that, it says a lot about the value of the content that is being linked to, and by extension about the brand behind it.

It is always worth remembering that links serve two purposes – they help with SEO, but they also bring actual visitors to your site, and It is possible that a link which would not carry much weight with search engines could be very valuable as a traffic builder. So, It is important to develop a strategy that identifies and prioritizes the links that you want to pursue.

Generally speaking, there are three different types of backlinks to your site:

"Natural links": These are backlinks that others create to your site of their own accord because they like your content and want to recommend it to their audiences. You really do need compelling and valuable content for this to happen, and perhaps to get the word out to a few appropriate influencers, but once you have some traction, these links are very efficient because you do not need to do anything more proactive to obtain them.

You may not know in advance that a natural link is being created, but It is always a nice gesture to thank the writer or site owner if you find a new link to your site. Unfortunately, there are times when a natural backlink is actually detrimental to your SEO because it comes from a poor-quality site, or perhaps is even being deliberately used as a malicious "black hat" tactic to undermine you.

Manually built links: These are backlinks that you research and directly solicit on an individual basis. They might be from current customers, influencers, or other sites with high authority that you decide to approach. Gaining these types of links can be extremely valuable, but the process takes time and involves nurturing relationships with site owners, requiring some people-oriented skills in addition to technical knowledge.

Self-placed links: In the past, it was common to place links yourself onto other sites, such as keyword-optimized press releases, writing guest articles and blog posts, and adding blog comments. These practices became so abused and spam-prone that search engines now frown on them, and many are viewed as black hat.

The relative value of different backlinks in an SEO context is known as link equity, also referred to as 'link juice.' This refers to the perceived value and authority that each backlink passes to your website. The thinking behind this is that if established and high-quality sites proactively endorse other sites, then those sites must be high-quality too. Lower quality sites therefore pass lower levels of link equity because their "word" counts for less.

There are a number of factors that contribute to link equity, including link popularity, which is the number of links pointing to the page giving the link.

A link from a page that itself has 100 backlinks will be more valuable than one from a page with 50 backlinks.

Another hugely important factor is the relevance of the content on the page giving the link to the content on the page receiving it. The two must be clearly related for the link to have value.

Anchor text - the words used in the visible, clickable part of the link on the page – is another important factor. These are usually shown in a different color to the rest of the text, and bolded or underlined so that they stand out to visitors who may wish to follow the link. In general, you will not have much control over the anchor text used by other site owners when linking to your pages. However, It is always worth suggesting anchor text that you would like to be used when writing manual link requests, remembering that including keywords within anchor text is recommended, but not as important as employing brief, relevant, compelling copy that may prompt visitors to actually click the link.

Another contributing factor is so-called 'freshness': High quality and relevant pages continue to earn links over time. 'Stale' pages with no recent links will start to lose link equity, so It is important to keep your content up-to-date.

And finally, authority and trust: the value passed by any link is also heavily influenced by the authority of the domain and of the URL that it comes from.

Authority is a very important concept within SEO, so It is worth exploring properly here:

The overall credibility of a website and its pages play a major role in its SEO outcomes. Google used to provide a toolbar called "PageRank" which provided its assessment of authority, but this has been discontinued. In its place, SEO software company Moz has developed a set of metrics to measure the authority both of a domain (known as "domain authority") and of a specific URL within the domain (known as "page authority"). You can see these numbers for any page in the free Moz browser toolbar, and they are generally regarded as good comparative indicators of site SEO strength, since they are based on a consistent methodology.

These authority measures consist of a score between 1 and 100, on a logarithmic scale (which means that It is easier to improve from, say, 25 to 35 than it is to get from 45 to 55). Scores do fluctuate based on the latest data and tweaks to the algorithm as well as changes to other sites. In other words, if you improve but other sites do even better, you may not see your score go up... in fact, it may even go down! New sites will always start with a score of 1 and – hopefully - progress from there.

When working on improving your own domain or page authority, your main goal is not 'to get to 100'... which would be almost impossible anyway. Look at the scores for your key competitors and try to beat those instead. The best way to raise your score is to increase your links from other sites with high authority as well as your overall search optimization. But bear in mind that as we have just explained, there is no guarantee that any one action will work for you, so do not obsess about these numbers if you are otherwise getting good SEO results. As Moz says, "there is not necessarily a 'good' or 'bad' domain or page authority score."

LINK RESEARCH

Now that you understand the importance of links, their various types, and how the relative value of individual links is assessed, It is time we considered how to find good target links for your site for a manual 'link-building' campaign.

When approaching a manual link-building campaign, first you should identify any keywords, products, or services for which you do not currently rank well. Perhaps you have new products to highlight, or you have found that prospects are using search terms for which you have not previously optimized. Having a good list of targets will help to focus your thinking.

Next, you need to look for potential links. There are many ways to do this, so here are a few suggestions:

Use a prospecting tool: Several tools are available that provide a list of possible links in response to your input keywords. Whatever tool you settle on should not necessarily replace your own manual searching completely, but it is likely to produce a deeper list than you probably would, and to include some suggestions that you might not have come across.

Search manually: Of course, this is time-consuming, but if you have a good understanding of the influential sites or people in your field, you should put it to use! Look for a range of blogs, magazines, directories, customers, colleagues, or businesses that sell complementary products, professional organizations, academic institutions, recognized experts, and so on. Create your own seed list of sites and specific pages that include external links or guest postings.

Use news alerts: News alerts or brand monitoring services can be very helpful in letting you know when you have received coverage, especially text-only mentions that you could request to be converted into links. News alerts set for your keywords or primary topics can also produce ideas for possible link placements.

Social media postings: Search for your keywords on social media platforms to see who is posting content around your topics. Some of these people might be possible influencers for you to work with as well as simply link prospects...

Once you have a list of possible links, you need to prioritize them by researching their respective link equity to see how much value each one might pass to your site. There are many excellent tools available for finding this information, and many vendors offer free trials so you will have the opportunity to see which one works best for you.

In reviewing link equity, you are looking for pages on other sites that have:

Good domain or page authority: Be aware, there are not definitive 'good' or 'bad' numbers in this regard. However, as a general rule, try to find sites with above average authority in your industry, or at least with higher authority than you currently have. It is also worth checking on the age of the domain since those that have existed for a while and built their own SEO track record will generally rank better than new domains.

Search ranking: Obviously, It is preferable to obtain a link from a page that is already ranking for your target keyword.

Potential for mutual benefit: Since you are going to be approaching sites for links, you need to have something of value to offer them as well as seeing the benefit that they will bring to you.

A reasonable number of existing links: Because of the issue with 'link farms' - directory pages that host many links without a clear relationship or mutual purpose - in general, pages with fewer links in total will pass higher link equity to your site. There's no hard and fast rule here, but if you find yourself looking at two pages where the other factors are equal, go for the one with fewer links.

Potential qualified visitors: Always remember that links are not only beneficial in improving your SEO. You are also looking for sites that appeal to your target markets, and which are likely to be a good source of qualified referral traffic, which is to say – traffic that is likely to convert, or do business with you.

If any of the sites you are targeting ask for payment or a reciprocal link, you should be aware that this is against search engine guidelines unless there is a clear, content-based reason for reciprocal links.

One of the most useful features of link research tools is that - since they can be applied to any site - you can also use them to research the link strategies of your competitors. Look at competitor pages that are ranking well for your target keywords and notice how many links those pages have earned, where they come from, their anchor text, and their link equity. There is no reason you should not approach sites that have linked to your competitors... but only as long as you are comfortable that these links will be high quality and beneficial to you as well.

Overall, your goal is to focus on the quality of the links that you are targeting, rather than sheer numbers. One high quality backlink can be worth the combined link equity and SEO value of many more low-quality ones. Keep building on a steady and consistent basis even if you achieve your ranking goals to lessen the chance of being overtaken by competitors.

ACQUIRING AND MANAGING LINKS

In order to obtain high quality links, It is vital to have a robust and well-thought-out content marketing strategy which is closely aligned with your SEO tactics. That means ensuring that your content is fresh, well-written, and contains appropriate keywords, headlines, and optimized images so that it is positioned to appear in search results.

You also need to think about the types of content that are most likely to attract links in your field. This means primarily educational or newsworthy content, rather than sales- oriented material, that is of value to your target audience and which would persuade bloggers and other writers to link to you, as well as providing a good incentive to the sites that you will manually offer it to. Your own corporate blog is an excellent hub for this type of content which is often referred to as "linkbait."

When you are working on obtaining links manually, the tone of any email that you send is critical, especially in cases where you do not have an existing relationship with the site owner. Here is a classic example of a typical link request, and how not to do it:

As with any public relations request, your link pitch should be based on the desire to create a mutually beneficial relationship with the person that you are approaching. This means that you should write an individual, personalized request in each case. Here are some elements of a professional pitch:

Write to a named person: If you do not already know the name of the person that you are writing to, do some research to find it. Do not write to an unnamed "webmaster."

Read and refer to their content: Spend some time reading the site or blog that you are targeting and identify what about it makes a good fit with your content. Perhaps you enjoyed an article on their site, or review they published, so let them know about that. Also, make sure that they are open to linking with other sites or accepting external writers, and if they have any specific guidelines for pitches, follow them!

Offer specific value: Instead of vague references to your content, provide specific examples of what you think will be valuable to your target site's audience. If you have produced some content, such as a whitepaper, that you think would be of interest, then let them know where they can find it - or offer to send them a copy. However, do not attach unsolicited materials to your initial email.

Make it easy to follow up: Include all of the ways that you can be contacted and be clear about your next step. It may not always be appropriate to ask for the link in the initial contact – you will need to have a feel for this. If you do include your request, be specific about which page of their site you are looking at, and why.

Check your spelling and grammar: Even the most well-constructed pitch can be ruined by unprofessional writing standards.

When you send the email, think of a more creative title than "link request"… which is likely to hit the recipient's spam filter. Do not send a very similar pitch to many people at once, especially for high-value links… otherwise you risk devaluing the relationship. And if you do not receive a response, do not harass the person – one polite follow-up may be all right, but no more.

There is a real art to writing good pitches, but if you are able to obtain some good links and some good relationships from them, It is well worth honing your skills in this regard.

As you grow your 'link profile,' the name used to collectively describe all of the links pointing to your website, you may find that the majority of your links are going to very few pages, and that you have a number of pages that you would like to rank better, but which do not have many links. In this situation, there are a couple of options available to you beyond manual link-building alone...

Reinforce your internal linking: Internal links from the highly-ranked, highly-linked pages will pass link equity, so look for ways to increase your internal links to the pages that you want to work on. Remember that these links do need to be relevant and appropriate otherwise you will just dilute your efforts.

Improve your content: You can also try to increase the natural links to these pages. Take a look at the content of the successful pages and see if you can identify what was so successful in attracting attention and perceived value, and if this can be replicated in other places.

Expand existing link relationships: Try reaching out to sites that already carry links to your site to see if they would be willing to place additional links on or to other pages.

You should also be aware that whenever you remove pages on your site, you will lose the link equity from any existing backlinks to those pages. If you have valuable backlinks, you should use a "301 redirect" to point a page to an alternative destination in order to preserve the value of the links.

Over the years, "black hat" practitioners have developed tactics that aim to manipulate rankings by creating a lot of poor-quality links. These have included link farms, repetition, and keyword stuffing in links. In 2012 Google responded by introducing the "Penguin" update to its algorithms, which defined and penalized "spammy" links.

Penguin itself has been updated several times, and you should read Google's guidelines on link schemes if you need a detailed understanding of what constitutes 'bad link is from Google's perspective. These include any form of paid link, links that are exchanged for the sole purpose of link-building and without any other value, any use of automated services that might create links, and mass guest article or blogging schemes with a lot of keyword-rich anchor text.

If you are thinking that this sounds complicated and somewhat open to interpretation... you are correct! The best rule of thumb is to stick to links that clearly serve a purpose beyond SEO – that is, they offer value to people too. This is why editorial links – links that are reviewed and implemented by the site owner - are seen as the highest quality, because they endorse the surrounding content.

Not all links are created equal, and some links may actually harm your SEO efforts. If you come to suspect that there are poor quality links pointing to your site and potentially harming your rankings, there are a few steps that you can take:

Take an inventory of all inbound links: There are a number of tools that will report links to your site, together with an assessment of their toxicity. Google's Search Console also provides a downloadable list of links that It is found for your site.

Manual requests: Just as you can request that individual links to your site be added to other sites, you can also ask for suspect or undesirable links to be removed. Of course, whether this happens or not is ultimately up to the site owner...

"Disavowing" links: Google provides a tool that you can use to upload a file of links that you want to be ignored in terms of passing any link equity or penalties to your site. However, we should stress that Google themselves recommend using this tool carefully since you do not always know whether a link is considered as spam or not. In fact, Google will automatically ignore links to your site that are clearly part of a hostile scheme that is out of your control.

"Nofollow" tag: This is a tag that can be added to links to instruct search engines not to pass link equity or SEO value to the destination page. This tag is useful when you want to include links on a page - to encourage click-throughs by visitors - but which you know might be problematic from a link spam perspective, such as comments on blog postings, or paid advertising or sponsor promotions.

Overall, if you are following a high-quality link strategy and you are happy with your link profile, you should not need to worry about these issues unless you experience a sudden drop in rankings and suspect that this may be due to some form of 'link spam.'

SEO FOR ECOMMERCE

I n this chapter, we will pick up what we have learned so far to discuss SEO specifically in the context of eCommerce sites, to give you the advice that your site needs to beat the competition and occupy lucrative positions on search engine results pages. Of course, everything we have already said about search marketing still stands, but we will look at how eCommerce sites might behave differently and which additional areas there might be for you to consider. Just remember that 'eCommerce SEO' is still fundamentally about creating a site that meets the needs of both your customers, and the search engines that help them to find you.

KEYWORD RESEARCH

It will come as no surprise that keyword research is particularly vital for eCommerce sites: because of the intense competition for lucrative keywords, but also because of the need to optimize product pages individually.

For your homepage or primary landing page – that is, the page where visitors arrive on your site - you will typically target keywords that have reasonable search volumes and levels of competition, together with high conversion potential. If that sounds a little non-specific, It is because this will be very context-dependent: you will need to understand your specific business, your target audience, and your competition.

As always, there are far more searches for short tail, generic keywords such as "cat food" than longer tail, more explicit phrases such as "organic chicken flavored cat food sachets." However, these high volume searches are usually highly competitive and tend to result in lower conversions because visitors have not yet narrowed down what they are really looking for, in other words: they might want to buy your cat food, but they might also be doing research for a school project about what you can safely feed to hedgehogs.

The more niche your product is, and the lower the level of competition, the more likely it is that you will get good results from shorter tail keywords. However, in competitive market places and with certain products you will often be forced to chase a longer tail of keywords, especially within the optimization of your individual product pages.

So, how do you start building out your keyword lists?

Firstly - if you are already running a paid search campaign, then take a close look at the performance of those keywords. Which ones attract high quality visitors who convert and otherwise interact with your content?

Reviewing competitor keywords and rankings is another helpful source of inspiration; either by using a research tool, or by looking directly at their sites, and observing how they organize their products and categories, and which words they use to describe them. However, It is crucial that you do not just copy what your competition does – there is no guarantee that what works for them will work for you, and you need to make sure that your keywords accurately reflect your offerings and your content.

Another quick tip here is that you can often find some great ideas by looking at the autofill feature on other prominent eCommerce sites. For example, type a search into Amazon for "cat food" and you will trigger a list of search queries that are, in part, informed by searches performed by others.

Of course, one of the most effective ways to gather insights on all aspects of eCommerce, including keyword research is to closely examine the behavior of your customers, and adjust accordingly.

At a minimum, you will have a host of data available to you from your site's own analytics, tracking users as they land on a page and then either move around your site or leave.

So, for example, if users are being directed to a page that screams "Buy Now!" but which does not provide much background or detail, they could easily "bounce" out again, with negative consequences for both revenue and SEO. This is exactly the sort of problem that will be visible to your analytics tools.

This is a big part of eCommerce SEO because although the primary goal and focus of your site is to persuade visitors to purchase, those searchers can enter your site at any point in their own journeys, so your SEO strategy must to take that into account. Careful attention to keywords can help you influence where different types of users "land" on your site, but this will never be perfect, so you need to provide them with clear options as to what to do next, no matter the circumstance.

After all, if they are ready to buy something… you want them to buy something with you now, but if they are not ready to do that just yet, you want them to get the information that they needed and come back later.

Gathering insights and drawing conclusions from the behavior of your visitors requires a grasp of the typical stages of purchase decision-making, referred to as the 'customer journey,' so we can examine the eCommerce SEO implications for each one:

First, there's awareness. At this stage, users do not yet know that you can meet their needs. They are looking for ideas about who can help them, and you want to appear in the mix of search results that they see.

The most common awareness stage search queries tend to be at the general category level, such as "kitchen pans," "bathroom designs" or "gifts for graduates." Ideally your site architecture should be built around categories of products, which is an opportunity to optimize for these more generic search terms.

Moving through to the consideration stage, visitors are conducting more in-depth research and narrowing down their choices. Their search queries tend to become a bit longer, looking for product reviews or comparisons, adding more specifics such as brand or color, or evolving into sub-categories, such as "non-stick frying pans" or "gifts for tech-savvy graduates." It can be difficult to tell the difference between these and awareness level searches, but the key point is that there is still no intent to make an immediate purchase.

At the decision stage, when users are ready to make an immediate purchase, their search terms will be for action words such as "buy" or "book," or very specific queries including elements such as product brand and name, size, model, or part number, and so on. For example, a search for "ASOS men's loafers navy size 10" would indicate a high buying intent. Your optimized individual product pages will be excellent for these types of searches.

Be careful using words like "discount," "cheap" and "deals;" they do signify buying intent, but they are also likely to lead to lower quality visitors who are less likely to make a purchase, and you need to consider whether you wish your brand to be positioned in this way. And of course, if you do not offer discounts or coupons, do not say that you do.

It can be difficult to actually identify the user intent driving every search by every user, but your own experience and data can still provide useful insights into how your specific customers search. The cost of a keyword in paid search can often tell you a lot about its associated buying intent: those with higher 'costs per click' often indicate higher buying intent because advertisers are willing to pay more for a more likely conversion.

It is quite possible that a user has already decided on the product that they want, but not where to buy it. In this instance, they could essentially be anywhere in the buying cycle, but your site itself, and those of your competitors, often becomes the focus of the decision rather than the individual item.

OPTIMIZING SITE CONTENT

The term 'site architecture refers to the layout of your site, and how you structure your navigation, category, and product pages. As with any site, this structure is critical in helping both visitors and search engine crawlers to understand what you have, and to find your products and supporting information quickly and easily.

Your site should be built in a horizontal - rather than a vertical - hierarchy, with main product categories, then sub-categories and then individual product pages. It should be scalable to allow for growth, and pages should be no more than three or four clicks from the homepage wherever possible. There is no "optimal" number of categories or sub-categories for eCommerce - the key is to design the most helpful user experience, although It is usually not a good idea to have a sub-category for individual products as search engines might have a low opinion of this.

Do not forget that you need to provide for all types of visitors, including those that just want to explore your offering and those that want to engage with any content that you provide... all the while without ever impeding those who are ready to skip straight to making a purchase.

Use your selected keywords in your URLs, categories, and filenames, and include breadcrumbs back up to the main category page for each product. Of course, product pages may well show up under several sub-categories.

Your homepage should link to all of the major category pages and best-selling product pages, and, internal linking should be used throughout linking related items and pages.

And as always in search, loading speed is extremely important, especially for mobile users, so be careful about adding too much third-party code to your pages. While it may improve the user experience or provide you with additional data, any benefits could be wiped out with a significant reduction in loading speed.

With all this in mind, we are going to take a look at optimizing individual pages, before focusing on specific locations such as category and product pages.

In general, with any individual page, you will want to include the primary keyword for that page in its URL, and wherever possible, make them short and readable. Visitors are more likely to click on a search result showing a URL that resembles their search, so something like this...

[petfoodsite.com/cat/dry-cat-food/furry-friends-kitty-kibble]

is, in general, a much better URL than this:

[petfoodsite.com/products/B06XDF6CT7]

For product pages in particular, try to include the primary keyword, as well as a few keywords related to features or benefits, in the title tag, and make sure to use a distinct and appropriate title for each page.

One of the key aims of SEO is to provide search engines with as much information as possible about your site and each of its individual pages. eCommerce is an area where it can be particularly important to make effective use of schema markup, this is code which helps Google to understand what your page is about by providing very specific additional information about the content in a standard metadata format, think of these like the page of publisher's information in a book; not that interesting to most readers, but very important to a librarian or collector.

Schema can provide data as routine as the name of the author of a web article, or as specialized as the weight and dimensions of a product, or whether a particular group of items on a restaurant's menu is suitable for vegans.

Remember: helping Google understand your offering will make them more confident about showing it to people. If someone is searching for "large rucksacks under 1kg" or "Vegan pasta in Rome" then the fact that you have provided that information could be critical.

Of course, the search engines will decide how and when they actually use the information, but they cannot use it if it is not there.

You can find lists of supported schema at the website schema.org, and Google offers a tool called the "Structured Data Markup Helper" that you can use to add the code to your pages.

If visitors find your category pages, they will have access to all of the products within that category. So, optimizing these pages is very beneficial for more general searches at the awareness or consideration stage of the buying cycle.

Think of your category pages as similar to the catalogues used by high street retailers. Visitors will use them as a starting point for navigation. If they cannot find an item using the category pages… they are likely to just assume that you do not stock it.

Each category page should begin with a description of what the category is and the types of products that it contains. This allows for the inclusion of internal links to sub- categories which are helpful for navigation and for indexing.

As well as the risk of a product being overlooked if users are looking for it in the wrong location, if there are too many inappropriate products in a category then the correct products can also be missed because of that. This makes assigning products to categories something of a balancing act. Put yourself in the user's shoes, and ask yourself where they would expect to see the product listed. Remember that items can be on more than one category page at the same time.

Individual product pages are an area where many eCommerce marketers really miss SEO opportunities, either by including little or no copy which leads to so-called "thin content" issues where the search engine cannot get enough information to understand the page... or by duplicating the same tired old product description from the manufacturer... which everyone else is using too...

In eCommerce, individual product pages are essentially where your sales pitch lives, and of course, getting your pitch right is critical.

This is where you should be creative - write your own description and try to make it unique. Think about your specific customers, and how they use each item, and create copy that speaks to them in a way that stands out. There is no specific rule about how long your copy should be, or what format it should take, but it should anticipate likely questions from potential buyers and incorporate the keywords for the page in as natural a way as possible.

Photos and video are powerful ways to convey messages about your products. Remember that search engines can struggle with images so you need to use appropriate keywords in image titles and alternative text tags, which are displayed if an image cannot be shown.

Include customer and editorial reviews, testimonials, ratings and trust seals as persuasive credibility and conversion rate boosters, particularly for lesser known brands.

When a product is out of stock, or you have temporarily stopped selling it, do not delete the page as you will risk losing any SEO traction that you have already gained. Instead, make sure that you have updated the page with a suitable message letting customers know what to expect.

Duplication issues can cause a lot of problems on these pages, and It is important to confront these head on. You might have more than one page about a specific product (in different categories, for instance), or a number of pages which are all slight variations on the same product. There is a variety of onsite techniques that you can use to deal with this.

As always, It is vital to ensure the overall user experience is great. Make sure text is clear and legible no matter what device is used, provide an intuitive mobile interface, with photos that can be tapped or swiped to access specific items, and, of course, a fast and straightforward checkout process.

There is one more aspect of individual pages that we should comment on here: due to eCommerce sites often presenting a large and ever-changing array of products, URLs may be generated as 'dynamic pages.' This is simply to say that they display different content depending on when and how they are accessed, and even by whom, but this can throw up some SEO issues - the main of which being that dynamic pages cannot be indexed properly. There are various technical workarounds for this, such as creating 'master' versions of these pages that can be indexed; and ensuring your sitemap is kept up-to-date is as important as ever in this context.

Another thing that can easily be overlooked is internal site search. Visitors often prefer to use a search utility over using category pages or following internal hyperlinks to find products.

And yet… this is another area where eCommerce sites often fall short, which can be very costly. After all, you cannot buy something if you cannot find it… So, It is possible that a 'mistake' would result in losing what would otherwise be an almost certain sale. In fact, research tells us that over 80% of shoppers will abandon a site if they have a poor search experience…

Provide a site search box. This may sound obvious, but It is important to include a prominent search box with a background that is distinct from any other input areas and in the same place on every page. Inserting placeholder text within the search box (for example "search by style, size or color") can also increase engagement and usage rates.

Use autocomplete. Displaying a list of the most likely completed searches as shoppers are typing their query is very helpful in avoiding spelling mistakes, and can often lead to visitors discovering products that they might not otherwise have been aware of.

Think about language. Most visitors will assume that their spelling and word usage is correct, so It is important to account for all possible variations to avoid errors. If visitors are using different words - or even just misspellings - for a product, you could add those to your synonyms list, to ensure they all return the same results.

With this in mind, keep an eye out for cases where no valid results are returned to the user. These are frustrating for shoppers, and you should study the types of search that cause this in order to minimize occurrences. And if searches are for products that are within your scope but which you do not currently carry, that is valuable market research as to what your customers expect from you!

And finally, allow customized filtering and sorting options. This is especially important on mobile screens, where sometimes only one or two search results will display at a time, and users will quickly lose interest when presented with a long list to scroll through. Allow users to apply filters such as price range, brand, color, size, review ratings, and so on... and also to sort results - for example, from highest to lowest price. Keep the search query and filters visible on the results page so that users can further refine their search criteria as they wish.

Visitors who search within your site usually already have a good idea of what they are looking for, so It is vital that your site search helps them as far as possible, and removes any obstacles that might be in the way of getting them to their objective.

LINK BUILDING FOR ECOMMERCE

Ensuring that your site and its individual pages are optimized is incredibly important, but there is more you can do to give yourself the edge over the competition.

SEO success, especially in the hyper-competitive world of eCommerce, demands that you consider all of the ways in which your site will be evaluated, and hyperlinks are still part of this. The presence of links will bring visitors to your storefront directly, with all of the downstream SEO benefits that this entails, but in addition: links from authoritative and respected sites represent a powerful vote of confidence in you that will not be overlooked by web crawlers.

First of all, you need content on your site that will motivate your audiences to engage with, write about and share with others. If you have the budget, include interactive features that allow visitors to discuss, engage with and share your products. Immersive video provides the ability for prospective buyers to imagine what an experience might be like far more effectively than words can convey; wish lists can also help encourage them to bring their friends on board.

Blogs can be excellent vehicles for attracting links, and It is well worth considering one for your eCommerce site. You can work with a variety of content types for this, including "evergreen" material that does not need to be changed very often, such as "how to" videos, usage instructions, and buyers' guides. Guest postings that you contribute to other prominent sites can also bring credibility and expand your audience, even if you need to use "nofollow" tags on any links that they contain – just remember that those links will still bring new visitors to your site... which will in itself provide SEO and revenue benefits.

When your content is ready, you will need to research and approach appropriate sites. For eCommerce sites, you might pay particular attention to:

- Competitor backlinks. It is always a good idea to take a look at where your competitors are getting their best links. Do not assume that all of their links will be beneficial to you, but even if the link location is unusable, research like this can reveal effective strategies.

- Influencers. Industry experts, social influencers and well-known reviewers who are followed by your target audiences can all be very powerful in generating links and traffic to your site.

- Directories and resource pages. Curated listings of resources and industry reviews can be relatively easy to obtain links in, although this should be limited to those directories that you expect to bring human traffic to your site.

- Related products. Businesses that sell related products to yours can be good sources for mutually beneficial links. For example, a winery might link with glassware suppliers, wine coolers or cheeses.

- Social media monitoring. Do not forget to follow what is being said about your brand on social media. Engaging in conversations could generate further links and reviews. And, if you have a large following, it might also be possible to build a community around discussions of your products, which would naturally generate a lot of buzz.

Done properly, link building can be a daunting prospect. It is time-consuming and very much a long-term strategy, but those links will bring paying customers to your site, and if you want to give yourself the best chance of success, you will need to employ every technique available to you.

SEO FOR MOBILE

I t almost goes without saying that more and more of us are accessing the digital world from mobile devices. But how does mobile's ever-rising presence impact upon search engine optimization? And how can you ensure you are reaching prospective customers, whether they are on desktop or on mobile? To answer these questions and more, in this chapter we will be focusing on SEO for mobile devices.

Before we get started, It is important to note that we will mostly be talking about search in the context of Google in these pages. Google is even more globally dominant in search on mobile than it is when all device types are taken into account – around 95% of mobile searches across the world are performed on its platform! And since we will mostly be talking about Google, we should also clarify that it does not consider tablets to be mobile devices, so we will be focusing, specifically on smartphones.

MOBILE SEARCH BEHAVIOR

Before we dive into the ins and outs of mobile SEO, It is crucial to recognize that optimizing for search on mobile will be of varying importance across different organizations and industries; and you should first understand how to work out how much of a priority its implementation should be for your business.

To do this, you will need to consider the specific behaviors of your visitors. Analytics data can be a great tool for this: study your analytics carefully to find out the proportion of your visitors using mobile devices, and what types of actions they take on your site. It is true that in most cases, more visitors are using smartphones than desktop for their online experiences. However, this is not always the case. There are instances, for some B2B companies, for example, in which search behavior is changing less quickly due to the nature of visitor's needs, which are often centered on in-depth research, complex information or viewing detailed specifications.

Beyond mobile's role within your visitors' search behaviors, mobile's role within SEO as a whole is also changing. As the use of mobile devices overtakes that of desktop, Google is moving to a "mobile-first" approach in indexing websites. This means that although Google will continue to maintain one index for both your desktop and your mobile sites, It is switching to considering the mobile version of a site as the primary one.

So, how exactly is search on mobile any different from search on desktop? Well, one key difference can be found in search behavior. Visitors tend to behave differently on mobile compared with desktop browsers – in fact, a recent study found that nearly 80% of searches were different across mobile and desktop. Whilst desktop users are more likely to dig deeper into a topic and be at an earlier, informational stage of the customer journey; mobile users are focused on one outcome at a time, and are more likely to be at a transactional stage.

In general, searchers on mobile are looking to fulfil an immediate need, which Google refers to as "micro-moments." These are split up into four main categories:

The first is "I want to know." Here, the user is looking for answers to questions. However, these questions are not necessarily about purchasing decisions, or implying any readiness to buy.

"I want to go" searches involve users looking for directions to a specific location, or looking for something "near me."

Then, there's "I want to do" searches, in which users are looking for help or ideas in carrying out a specific task.

And finally, "I want to buy" searches indicate a user is looking to make a purchase.

Google prioritizes those sites which provide the most relevant and valuable content for any given search. As a result, there can be significant differences between rankings and results pages for the same keyword on both mobile and desktop.

When a user makes a search on mobile, Google's algorithm tries to establish which type of micro-moment is happening in order to display appropriate results. So, whilst an "I want to know" search might generate an answer box or a featured snippet, an "I want to go" search might instead generate a local map pack.

All types of mobile searches have increased significantly, and searchers are more receptive to marketing messages when looking for in-the-moment answers and solutions, so It is worth looking closely at your mobile search queries to find patterns of user intent and tailoring the appropriate content to satisfy these micro-moments. If you find your visitors have "I want to do" type needs, for example, you might want to use video content, which can be particularly helpful in showing users how to carry out a specific task.

However, mobile search behavior is not completely clear-cut. Whilst typed mobile search queries tend to be shorter due to smaller screens and keyboards, voice searches – that is, searches that are made by users speaking their search query – are often formed of complete sentences, and are therefore generally longer. This can be somewhat confusing: although you can segment search queries by device in Google Analytics, unfortunately you cannot currently distinguish between typed and spoken mobile searches.

Understanding search behavior is crucial for successful SEO, no matter the device. In order to optimize your site and your content for mobile devices, It is vital to first develop an understanding of both mobile's role within your audience's search behavior and within SEO as a whole.

OPTIMIZING FOR MOBILE

Key to any SEO effort is ensuring that your site provides a user-friendly experience, and mobile SEO is no exception.

When designing your mobile site, you have three main options.

The first is to use a mobile website. Hosted at a different URL, usually with the subdomain "m." as opposed to "www.," this is a completely different set of files and design from the desktop site.

Alternatively, you might use dynamic serving. Here the server detects the user's device type and returns content tailored to that device. Like mobile sites, the files served are different, however this time the URL remains the same across mobile and desktop.

And finally, there's responsive design. In this scenario, there is only one URL and only one set of files. However, the coding and style sheet make the content adaptable so that it displays appropriately across devices.

When using responsive design, you will want to use the "viewport" meta tag. The viewport refers to the viewing area of the visitor's screen, which will be smaller on mobile than on desktop. This tag tells the browser how to control the page's dimensions and scaling so the size of the page can be adjusted according to the visitor's device.

Google's recommended setting for this tag looks like this:

```
<meta name="viewport" content="width=device-width, initial-scale=1.0">
```

... and is very clear that with "mobile first," responsive design is the preferred choice. In fact, It is now considered best practice to first design pages for an optimal mobile experience, and then allow the responsive code to adapt the content to work for desktop users.

When it comes to providing an optimal mobile experience, there are a number of factors you should consider.

One major aspect is loading speed. "Dwell time," or the amount of time visitors spend on a given page before returning to the results page, is a major ranking factor – according to Google, over half of visitors abandon a mobile site if it takes more than 3 seconds to load.

You should also consider whether elements on your pages are user-friendly – are phone numbers clickable? Can text be read without zooming? Is the content appropriately sized for small screens? Are links placed far enough apart that the correct one can be tapped? You should also ensure that there are no crawl errors on the site which might prevent full indexing.

In order to assess the speed and usability of your mobile site, there are plenty of tools available to help you with this, such as those provided by Google.

For example, the "mobile friendly" test offered through Google's web console provides an assessment of how user-friendly your mobile site is, the "mobile speed test" can highlight any problems with load time, and the "smartphone" option can be used to identify any crawl errors in the mobile version of your site – including whether the viewport meta tag has been correctly configured.

Each of these tests will give you a rating and a detailed list of recommendations for improvements where applicable. This might include avoiding the use of Flash, compressing images, or making code alterations. These improvements can be quite technical, so your web team are probably best placed to handle them – if you do run these tests, make sure that you communicate your findings to the appropriate parties.

When it comes to optimizing your content for search, many SEO best practices apply equally to mobile: creating valuable and well-written content with compelling titles, descriptions, and calls to action; including an XML sitemap and strong internal links; and working on a robust inbound link-building strategy.

However, there are still some steps that you should take to optimize specifically for mobile search.

Firstly, do mobile-specific keyword research. It is vital to understand your successful mobile keywords (that is, those that attract visitors who best support your goals), because an effective use of SEO will employ a separate mobile strategy. Google Analytics' mobile- only traffic segment can be particularly helpful here.

Next, consider your titles and meta descriptions. Because of the smaller screen on mobile, It is possible that your titles or descriptions may be cut short. To persuade searchers to click on your link, include the most important words at the beginning.

And finally, there is a correlation between social signals and SEO rankings, so you will also need to think about the mobile aspect of social sharing. Assuming that they are used by your target audience, include buttons for sharing on the most commonly used mobile messaging platforms, such as Facebook Messenger or WhatsApp.

But remember, above all, It is vital to provide valuable content. It can be easy to fall into the trap of removing some of the more niche, in-depth content from your mobile site because you are worried that it may be too much. However, doing this in the "mobile-first" era may have the effect of removing this valuable content from the view of Google's crawlers, preventing it from appearing in search results.

As with any SEO campaign, a key element of successful mobile SEO is monitoring outcomes – for example where you are ranking for relevant searches - and implementing steps for continuous improvement.

Because of the differences in mobile and desktop search behavior, Google uses different algorithms for each device type in order to generate the results pages that are most relevant to the user. This means that your site may rank differently on mobile than it does for the same keyword on desktop.

If you rank lower for the same keyword on mobile than you do on desktop, look for any clues as to the cause. A good place to start is assessing the user experience of your site – is your bounce rate, or the proportion of users who arrive and then immediately leave, for these pages higher on mobile than it is on desktop? If so, this might indicate that the content works better for desktop visitors, or that visitor intent for the keyword differs between devices. For example, a search for a specific product on a mobile device may mean "where can I buy this near here?" – so It is unlikely that a non-local eCommerce site would fit the bill. However, on desktop, this type of site may better suit the user intent, and may therefore be placed more prominently within the search results.

One way of accessing this information is to use the Search Console Queries report. By adding device type as the 'secondary dimension,' you can compare the average position for the same keyword on desktop, mobile and on tablet; and a number of other major SEO tools also allow you to see your rankings for both desktop and mobile separately.

You should also evaluate the quality of the mobile traffic that arrives as a result of your SEO efforts. Google Analytics can be particularly helpful here: create a custom segment of mobile visitors from organic search, and compare the volume, behavior, and conversions of these visitors with other segments, such as with non-mobile organic search visitors, or mobile non-organic search visitors.

Here, you are looking for any interesting patterns or trends that might offer insights into whether your mobile SEO visitors are well-qualified for your site, the landing pages that they are seeing are appropriate, they are converting at the same rates and are spending at the same levels, and so on. And of course, you should use your mobile traffic segments to evaluate these visitors against the specific KPIs that you have set for your SEO campaigns.

NEW DEVELOPMENTS

As technology develops, the SEO landscape is evolving and advancing with it, and mobile search is no exception.

One key development that is hard to ignore is voice search. With the advent of Siri, Cortana, Alexa, and Google's unnamed voice assistant - and with the growth of mobile search in general - voice (or spoken) search is predicted to grow to over half of all searches in the next couple of years!

When a user makes a voice search, instead of a selection of results to choose from, the algorithm selects just one answer to deliver to the user. So, what can you do to give yourself the best chance of appearing in that answer?

Well, understanding featured snippets is key here. These are the boxes that appear at the top of results pages which contain the answer to the search question sourced from a web page, and include the web page's URL and title. This should not be confused with the answer box, which gives a concise response to a clear question that has only one answer - "What time is it in New York?" - but does not provide an associated website.

The featured snippet is often the result that is read aloud by the voice assistant in response to a spoken query, so to optimize for voice search, you will need to optimize for featured snippets.

Voice searches tend to be focused on areas such as immediate information or purchase needs, directions, and entertainment. And because spoken searches tend to use conversational language - generally speaking, longer than a typed search - this can be an excellent area in which to review your most successful long-tail keywords. Featured snippets are typically displayed in response to informational searches, so look for the questions that are most frequently asked by current and potential customers about your products and services. To do this, you should consider reviewing your analytics reports, using a keyword suggestion tool, or... why not check in with your sales and customer support teams who could provide some valuable input.

When you have a list of questions, try typing them into a search engine to see what the current featured snippet looks like. Can you fill any gaps in the information or improve on it in some other way? If so, consider creating a blog post or page that answers the question directly and adds any further detail that you can provide. Q&A or numbered bullet point structures can be particularly helpful in optimizing for featured snippets because they break the content up into smaller logical chunks for the voice assistant to read. Do not worry about including too much content - if you do achieve this spot, the box will include a link to your site.

The algorithms powering voice search are proprietary, and we are still at the early stages of understanding how to optimize for voice. However, domain authority and page loading speed appear to have an impact on voice search results, and, according to recent studies, adding structured data markup is very helpful in optimizing for featured snippets.

Voice search does work a little differently, but It is still based very much on understanding user intent, providing quality in-depth content and a great visitor experience. Even though the initial search is through voice, there is always a possibility that users will be interested enough in your answer to dive deeper into your website, and if that results in a lot of immediate bounces, you will not hold the top slot for long!

Beyond developments in how users are searching, we should also touch upon advancements in the types of mobile site available that aim to improve user experience.

Recently, Google and Twitter have launched an open source project called Accelerated Mobile Pages with the goal of improving the loading speed of mobile pages. It is essentially a stripped-down version of HTML – JavaScript is not allowed, images do not load until you scroll to them, and It is very easy for Google to store and serve your content without needing to go back to your site.

Opting for Accelerated Mobile Pages can be a great choice. Firstly, they are prominently displayed in mobile results pages and can include images to attract more attention. They are even accompanied by a small thunderbolt icon which distinguishes them from other pages, and lets users know that these results will load faster. Some Google results pages also feature an Accelerated Mobile Page carousel, in which multiple pages are displayed in a horizontally-scrolling row which is far more eye-catching than the standard title, description, link, and so on...

As well as loading faster, which can make a huge difference to the mobile user experience and in turn, decrease bounce rates, they also use less data.

However, there are of course some reasons you might be hesitant about choosing Accelerated Mobile Pages. For a start, there are strict guidelines about what can and cannot be included. For instance, you cannot use pop-ups to invite visitors to join your email list or run an on-site survey; if you host advertising you may lose revenue; and you will have to do some additional set-up for analysis tracking. But above all, you will need to maintain two sets of pages: one Accelerated Mobile Page, and one that includes all of the elements that cannot be included in that version; meaning extra costs, content management and updating concerns.

Whether you decide to use Accelerated Mobile Pages or not is an individual decision. It is early in its history, so it remains to be seen whether it will become widely adopted, whether other developments such as 5G will render it unnecessary, and how Google will continue to handle sites that use it or not. It is clearly beneficial to high-traffic sites, but if you are a smaller business with fewer resources, or if you are satisfied that your site is sufficiently optimized for mobile and loads quickly, then you may choose to forgo the extra effort.

Alternatively, you might instead want to use Progressive Web Apps. These are essentially websites which offer an "app-like" experience, but from within a standard browser – including on desktop. Progressive Web Apps load quickly, have responsive design to fit any device and screen size, and allow for some basic navigation even when Wi-Fi signal is unavailable. And like native apps, they offer push notifications to alert users of new products, offers, events, and so on.

As with Accelerated Mobile Pages, Progressive Web Apps are in the very early stages of development – not many business are using them yet, and there are still some issues with specific browsers and operating systems. However, many experts are predicting their use will grow as they seem to offer the best of both the mobile web and mobile apps. For example, you do not need to develop different versions of a website for various operating systems, and no app downloads are involved. Importantly, the major advantage of Progressive Web Apps is that they can be crawled for indexing in the same manner as a web page, and do not require the additional steps needed to optimize a native app.

Keeping up with advancements like these will allow you to put your best foot forward in reaching mobile searchers. The SEO landscape will continue to change and develop, and It is your job to evolve and adapt with it.

CLASSIC BLACK-HATS TECHNIQUES

In the ever-evolving world of search engine optimization (SEO), maintaining ethical standards is essential to ensure your website's long-term success. Search engines like Google continuously update their algorithms to provide users with the most relevant and trustworthy search results. Consequently, black hat SEO techniques, which seek to manipulate search engine rankings through deceitful means, often face harsh penalties.

In this chapter, we will explore some classic black hat SEO tactics that have fallen out of favor due to the consequences they entail.

In the SEO landscape, ethical practices are the bedrock of long-term success and credibility. While black hat SEO techniques may promise short-term gains, they come with significant risks, including penalties, loss of trust, and damage to online reputation.

To build a strong online presence, focus on white hat SEO strategies. Create high-quality content, earn natural backlinks, and prioritize user experience. By adhering to Google's guidelines and consistently delivering value to your audience, you can achieve lasting success in the competitive world of search engine optimization.

LINK FARMS

We are already talked briefly about link farms. Once a favored method for artificially inflating a website's backlink count, link farms involved websites linking to each other indiscriminately, often without relevance. This practice aimed to create the appearance of authority in the eyes of search engines.

However, Google now categorizes link farms as a severe violation of its guidelines. Engaging in link farm activities can lead to significant penalties, including a drop in search rankings or even complete de-indexing.

CLOAKING

Cloaking: Cloaking is a deceptive technique wherein a website displays different content to search engine crawlers than what is shown to human visitors. This discrepancy aims to achieve high search engine rankings while presenting users with irrelevant or low-quality content. Google actively penalizes websites employing cloaking methods, as they disrupt the search engine's ability to deliver valuable and relevant results. Consequences may include lower rankings or removal from search results.

KEYWORD STUFFING

Keyword stuffing is the practice of overloading a webpage with excessive keywords, often in an unnatural and unreadable manner. The objective is to deceive search engines into ranking the page higher for those keywords. Google's algorithms have grown sophisticated enough to detect keyword stuffing. Engaging in this practice can result in keyword-based penalties, harming a website's search engine rankings and credibility.

DUPLICATED CONTENT

Duplicate content involves copying content from other websites or duplicating one's own content across multiple pages. This practice can dilute the quality of search results by offering redundant information to users.

Google aims to provide users with diverse and valuable content. Websites with duplicate content may face ranking penalties, as Google may choose to display only one version of the content or demote the site altogether.

HIDDEN CONTENT

Hidden Text and Links: Hidden text and links involve manipulating a webpage's code to conceal keywords or links from users while making them visible to search engines. These tactics are used to increase keyword density or create artificial internal links. Google considers hidden text and links as deceptive practices and penalizes websites employing these techniques. The penalties can negatively impact a site's visibility in search results.

PART II
PAID SEARCH

PAID SEARCH

Paid search ads appear on the results pages of search engines like Google or Bing, on shopping sites such as Amazon, or on social media platforms like Facebook and Pinterest.

In this series of chapters, we will be focusing on Google, the most popular search engine globally with over 5 billion searches performed there every day. We will be looking specifically at Google search campaigns, from establishing your goals and objectives, to deciding on a budget, to exploring how you go about setting up your Google Ads account - which is where you will manage all of your PPC activity. We will also explore how to research and choose your keywords and how to go about writing your ad copy and ad extensions.

WHAT IS PAID SEARCH?

Paid Search is all about getting your products or services to the top of the results page when a user makes a search. It is also known as 'Pay per Click,' or PPC, which is the buying method used in this type of advertising where brands bid to have their ad shown to a user whose search query indicates that they have an interest in something relevant to that brand.

It provides the perfect opportunity to be in the right place, at the right time and to deliver relevant and useful messages to users who are actively seeking the products and services you offer.

A user enters a query into a search engine, for example: 'buy birthday cake in Paris' and the search engine identifies all the brands that are currently bidding on keywords related to that query. In this case, these keywords might be 'birthday cake,' 'party' or just 'cake.'

Next, advertisers bidding on those keywords are entered into an auction. There are a number of factors that determine which ads are shown to searchers and where they appear on the results page. These include: how much you are willing to pay when an user clicks on your ad, the ad extensions you use, your Quality Score - which is a metric that Google uses to determine how useful or relevant your ad will be to the user - and your Ad Rank - a formula that determines which ads are shown on the results page.

So far, no money has changed hands but this changes if a user clicks on your ad, hence the name 'Pay Per Click.' The user will arrive on a landing page that should provide them with more information regarding their search query and - in most cases - then move further down the path to purchase.

That is a simplistic look at how the paid search ecosystem works and how ads appear on the results page. It is a complex process that is affected by a number of moving parts - some of which you might already be aware of. Google also makes changes to Google Ads frequently, so It is advisable to review the latest updates before you implement any PPC campaigns.

If all this is new to you however, do not worry. Over these sections, we will help you build a whole picture of PPC, from how to choose ad copy and keywords, to exploring what Ad Rank is and how you can use different bidding strategies to affect how much you spend at auction.

But, before we explain all of that, It is important to first look at how you set goals for your paid search activity. For this, you should bear in mind that the ultimate purpose of this type of advertising is not to just gain clicks, but to support your overall business objectives: a click on your paid search ad is just one step along the customer journey.

There are many business goals that can be helped by PPC, but improving brand awareness is a common one. This is especially the case if your business is relatively new, or if you are aiming to increase the number of people who have heard of your company.

Increasing website traffic is also a typical goal for PPC activity. Now, this is not just about increasing the number of visitors to your website: you do not want to spend money bringing unqualified visitors to your site who will never become customers. Always think of your target audience and the customer journey - you want to pay for website visitors who are in a buying mindset, or who are seriously searching for a product or service that you offer.

Finally, increasing sales and revenue are key objectives for most PPC campaigns. The idea here is that paid search campaigns should generate a good rate of conversion, which in turn should generate more leads and therefore more sales, directly impacting your bottom line.

It is worth bearing in mind at this point that PPC advertising is not ideal for every business out there, and It is certainly not appropriate in every situation. The majority of searchers use search engines to obtain information and they are rarely immediately intending to buy - so if you are solely focused on conversions you will need to monitor your results carefully to avoid overspending without meeting your goals. And if you are focused predominantly on brand awareness, or if you are not interested in immediately making sales, then you need to be comfortable that your expenditure is justified.

Once you decide on your goals, you will need to determine a budget for your paid search activity. There are a few ways you can go about doing this.

If you are already using Google Ads, you can analyze your past performance to help determine an appropriate budget. Use your goals to ascertain which of your campaigns are delivering and which are not. Campaigns that are hitting targets might benefit from having a little more spent on them -

especially if you are getting good conversion rates but not many impressions.

Google's Keyword Planner can also help businesses to work out a budget for paid search activity. It shows you the projected cost for each keyword you are bidding against based on its current search volume, and shows how your click through rate might change depending on how much you bid on a particular keyword. By comparing these numbers with your goals, you should be able to establish a potentially worthwhile budget.

When you are first starting out, your paid search campaigns will require a lot of testing and optimization - and that goes for your budget as well as your ads. The good news is that you can change your expenditure at any time in response to your ad performance, and you should monitor new campaigns closely to see if your money is being well spent.

Once you have decided on a budget and your goals, you will need to set up an Ads account. Now, the structure and settings of your account can really impact your ability to manage your campaigns efficiently, so It is important to understand the hierarchy in place in Google Ads' accounts and best practices when it comes to setting them up.

First, the very top level: your overall account. Here, you will define user access permissions, enter billing information, and contact details for your account, as well as choosing the display language and number format. It is here you can also link to Google Analytics - Google's website analytics platform - and the Google Search Console - a service that helps you monitor and troubleshoot your site's presence in Google's search results.

Within your Ads account you will create multiple campaigns, which you will use to organize your ads into logical categories, with each campaign focusing on specific keywords and ads. It is at the campaign level that you will set up targeting parameters such as location and the different devices on which you want your ad served. You will also set a daily budget for each campaign.

There are many different ways to structure your campaigns and decide on what each campaign should focus on. Some brands choose to structure their campaigns based on the structure of their website, or sometimes they might choose to structure them around the locations they wish to target, the different stages of the customer journey

or their different product offerings. A store that sells denim clothing might set up campaigns for their jackets, skirts, and jeans, for example.

Once you have set up your campaigns and decided on targeting parameters and budgets, you will need to turn your attention to the next level in the Ads account hierarchy: Ad Groups.

Your Ad Groups are where you will keep track of the keywords, ads, and landing pages you create for specific campaigns.

Good Ad Group organization is essential for helping you manage your PPC activity, so do not rush this bit. Search engines partly decide which ads to show to searchers based on the keywords and ad copy in your Ad Groups – so if they do not really match a searcher's query, your ad might not be seen. The same goes for if you place the same keyword in multiple Ad Groups – if multiple ads have the same keyword, Google might choose the wrong ad to show for an individual's search.

Because of this, you should ensure that your Ad Groups are specific – they should not be too generic or try to target too many search queries. For example, if you are a bakery, you might create different campaigns in your Ads account for the different products you sell, like 'cakes,' 'doughnuts' and 'bread.' Under the 'doughnuts' campaign, you should create separate Ad Groups for 'glazed doughnuts,' 'jam doughnuts' and 'churros,' rather than trying to advertise all of these different types of products in one Ad Group using a generic ad for 'doughnuts.'

Once you decide on your Ad Groups, you can then start to select keywords that will work for each individual Ad Group. Again, make sure that the keywords you add to each Ad Group are relevant – you should avoid making them too generic. For example, if you have an Ad Group for the churros you sell, you should not include keywords in your Ad Groups for jam doughnuts that would apply to search terms that refer to churros.

One technique for ensuring good Ad Group organization is to start out by creating your ads and associated landing pages. Then look at each keyword and see which ad is best suited to it. If a keyword does not closely relate to your existing ads, that is probably a sign that you need to create a new Ad Group.

It is easy to rush the setup of your Ads account, especially when you are eager to start creating the ads that will appear on the search results page. But taking your time and setting up your campaigns and Ad Groups in a logical fashion will really pay off later down the line, especially when you are looking to optimize your keywords, ads and landing pages and generate effective reports.

KEYWORDS

Now you know how to set up your Ads account, the steps you need to take to decide on a suitable budget and how to set your goals, It is time to explore one of the most important parts of setting up your campaigns: deciding on your keywords.

Effective use of keywords is central to your PPC strategy because they define when your ads will be shown - and when they will not.

Now, (Truck Left Begins Here) when we talk about keywords, It is important to ensure that you know the difference between search queries and keywords and how they relate to one another. Search queries or search terms are words or phrases that users type into search engines when they are searching for something. Whereas keywords are the words that you include in your campaigns and bid on to ensure that your ads are displayed to users when they perform a search query.

When a user performs one of the billions of searches that Google handles every day, Google checks to see whether their search terms match any of the keywords in your account - if there is a match, there is a chance that your ad may be shown on the results page. Because of this, you need to be very discerning about the keywords you choose and It is important to do some serious research in this area to ensure your ads are shown to the right customers, in their moment of need.

Before you begin defining your keywords, you will need a deep understanding of your target customers and their buying behavior. This will help you to consider the purchase intent behind each search query, which in turn should influence the ad copy and landing page you will use for each keyword.

The good news here is that different searches can give a very good indication of a user's intent...

Meet Andy. Andy is looking to purchase a new bike, but he is not really sure about the right bike for him, or where he can make a purchase. He turns to Google for help, with search queries like: 'what is the best bike for cycling to work?.' These are what are called informational searches, and indicate that while Andy is seeking information, he is not looking to make an immediate purchase. They are ideal for brands who wish to build long term relationships with their customers by providing them with information.

Once Andy has decided on the type of bike he wants, he starts searching Google using words and phrases that suggest he is ready to buy, like 'bikes for sale in New York' and 'buy second-hand bicycles in Manhattan.' These are what are called transactional searches and indicate that a searcher is in a buying mindset.

Branded searches are also a good indicator of a user's intent to make a purchase. These are search queries containing a brand name, meaning that a user has a clear idea of what they are looking for and even what they want to purchase.

Andy's queries have also included place names. Referred to as location searches, these are very popular, especially on mobile devices, and allow for precise targeting which makes them very useful to businesses that operate in specific areas.

Once Andy has purchased his bike he might also perform searches that use words that describe a problem. For instance, he might use search queries like 'flat tire' or 'faulty brakes' rather than 'bike repair shop.' These are called problem searches and, in these cases, It is important to use keywords that describe the problems that you solve, in addition to listing your products or services.

These different types of searches are not mutually exclusive - you might find someone performing a search that is both informational and transactional. Now, it can be almost impossible to be sure of user intent from one search query. Queries can be rather ambiguous, so be wary of making too many assumptions until you are able to learn from experience as you run your own campaigns.

So, now you know the type of searches users perform when using search engines like Google. But how do you actually go about deciding on the right keywords for your brand?

Well, first of all you need to think like your customers. Put yourself in their shoes - what words or phrases would they type to bring them to your website? If you were looking to purchase your own products or services, for what would you search?

Then, take a look at the landing pages that your ads will link to. Read each page and take keywords from each one - if your website is well put together, you should be able to get a pretty comprehensive list of keywords that directly link to the products or services that your business provides.

If your keywords are quite broad, make them more specific. For example, say your keyword is 'shoes.' You might want to specify 'children's shoes,' then 'children's sandals,' then 'children's red sandals.' There are merits to using broader keywords because they have higher search volumes but many advertisers go wrong in this area because they waste money bidding on generic, broad keywords that do not describe visitors' actual needs.

This kind of strategy, commonly referred to as generic search, can lead to high bounce rates, where high numbers of users leave a site immediately without having viewed the content on the page. This is not only a waste of money, but it tells Google that your ads are not relevant to searchers and could lead to your ad being shown less frequently on the results page.

Finally, consider researching different variations of your keywords. Users will not all utilize the same words to search for similar products and services, and your keywords should reflect that. Search engines are increasingly intelligent, but you should not rely on them to recognize the difference between 'earphones,' 'earbuds' and 'headphones,' for example. It is best to include variations and even synonyms in your keywords, since doing so means you are not relying on the search engine to do your work for you.

Once you have a list of all the keywords you want to use in your PPC campaigns, you then need to choose what is called a Keyword Match Type for each of them. Keyword Match Types essentially give Google direction about how assertive it should be when it matches your advertisements to user searches, and Google gives a number of different Match Types to choose from.

First, we will look at broad match keywords. Let us imagine you bid on the keyword 'wedding cake.' Broad match will allow a search engine to show your ad for any search it deems relevant. They have the greatest reach, but require you to have a large budget, because you will attract clicks from searchers who might not specifically be looking for your products or services. With a broad match for the keyword 'wedding cake,' your ad might also show for other wedding-related items and other types of special occasion, like birthdays, for which you might not offer services.

Broad match modifier, on the other hand, allows you to designate words that must be present in the search query, but still allows for other words or combinations. A broad match modifier for the keyword 'wedding cake' would prevent non-wedding or non-cake related searches from triggering your ad, but would allow for other permutations such as 'tiered wedding cake' or 'wedding cake for vegans.'

Phrase match only allows your ad to appear if the search query contains a certain phrase - for example, 'wedding cake for vegans' - which must appear in the word order that you specified, although other words can come before or after the phrase.

In this case, phrase match would allow your ad to show for the search query 'buy wedding cake for vegans' but not for the search query 'buy vegan wedding cake,' because your chosen phrase does not match this search.

Exact match is pretty simple: it requires that the search query be exactly the same as the keyword. This is the most restrictive match type and will yield the fewest clicks because it is so specific and your reach will most likely be small. However, because you can specify that your ads only show for certain keywords, exact match is useful if you have limited budget and wish to target only the most qualified visitors and only your top-performing keywords.

Finally, a word on negative keywords. There may be some keywords that would be inappropriate for your business goals, or that you have learned from experience do not convert. You can ensure that your ads are not displayed in these situations by defining negative keywords which will prevent an ad from being triggered if they appear in the search query. For example, if you make wedding cakes but do not yet make vegan wedding cakes, you could make 'vegan' a negative keyword.

If you opt for negative keywords you do need to be careful about excluding too much. Some eCommerce sites have been caught out by making 'free' into a negative keyword to avoid advertising to people hoping for free samples, but in doing so unwittingly blocked searches that included 'free shipping' which they did offer.

In practice, most experts advise using a mix of broad match modifier and exact match, as use of broad match alone can lead to a lot of wasted ad spend, and phrase match can be too restrictive as it can prevent your ads from showing for appropriate search queries, unless the word order of a search query is important. As always though, it depends on the amount of budget you have, your goals and objectives for PPC and the products and services that you are offering.

Ad Copy

Once you have decided on the keywords you want to bid on, you will need to come up with the ads users will see if they enter a query into the search bar and your ad wins a spot on the results page. The ads themselves are central to PPC campaigns and creating them can be quite tricky since you have limited space to attract the right clicks.

Google's text ads consist of three main components: the headline, the display URL, and the description text. The headline is the part of the ad that is displayed in blue and appears in a larger font than the rest of the ad. On Google you have 3 headlines of up to 30 characters each, which are shown on the same line, separated by a dash or vertical line character.

The display URL is shown under the headline and is used for ad copy purposes only -it does not necessarily have to match the URL of the landing page that a visitor will arrive at when they click on the ad. The display URL is made up of your domain and two optional path fields of up to 15 characters each. Google will decide whether or not to show the full URL, but it is worth creating a powerful one anyway because when it is shown it gives you more opportunity to advertise to a user.

Finally, the description text consists of up to 90 characters and should describe your offer and contain an effective call to action to persuade visitors to click on your ad. Google allows advertisers to include two descriptions in their ads.

So, you know what goes into an ad, but...how do you go about writing effective ad copy?

There are a number of things you can do to ensure your ad copy is in the best shape to advertise your products to potential customers.

First of all, leverage your keywords. Keywords appear in bold font and using them in your ad copy reassures users that your ad directly relates to their search query. However, beware of over-using them: test carefully to see if you get better results by placing your keywords in the headline, display URL or description text.

Using numbers and statistics is one way to make your ad copy stand out: prices, discounts, savings and proof of your product features or benefits are eye-catching and improve click-through rates. Your ads should also include a strong call to action, making it clear what you want users to do and what they will receive as a result.

Emotional triggers can also work well and Google even offers customization features like automated sales countdowns that can create a powerful incentive to purchase. You can also increase the emotional appeal of your ads by addressing the audience directly using words like 'you' and 'your.'

Finally, emphasize what makes you unique! Ads for similar products can look virtually the same, so it is important to underline what sets you apart from the competition, like unique product features or awards you have won.

Google has strict policies for ad copy, and each ad undergoes a review process by Google before it is eligible for display. Ads with poor grammar, spelling mistakes, incorrect use of punctuation or capitalization, vague statements or exaggerated claims can all be disallowed. There are also specific rules governing ads that deal with certain subjects, such as adult content, alcohol, guns and other dangerous objects, political ads, gambling, and healthcare. If you are promoting products in these categories, you will need to be familiar with the relevant guidelines.

Now, we have mentioned them a number of times but let us tackle them head on: landing pages. There's little point spending a great deal of time crafting your ad copy and researching the right keywords if your landing pages are not up to scratch.

Great ads that take visitors to disappointing landing pages will not only annoy your potential customers but they will lead to higher bounce rates and render all of the good work you did getting a user to click on your ad completely obsolete. Because of this, it is crucial that your landing pages live up to the promise of the ads that users click on. They must clearly convey information, have a compelling call to action, and make it easy for visitors to complete a desired action so that you are not wasting the money you spend getting them to your site in the first place.

Ideally, you would have a dedicated landing page for each Ad Group, but this could be a lot of work. At a minimum, make sure that each ad links directly to relevant content on your site. Do not make one of the most common PPC mistakes and send all visitors to your homepage - this will leave visitors having to search to find the content or products that they are looking for, and is one of the surest ways to get a high bounce rate and to lose money!

Always think of the customer and what they are looking for - if they have clicked on your ad, they are clearly indicating a need for something that you are offering, and it would be foolish to not give them what they are looking for in a clear and competent manner.

That brings us to the end of this chapter on PPC. Join us next time where we will be explaining what Ad Rank and Quality Score are, why they are so important and how you can improve them. We will also take you through the different targeting options and bidding strategies available to you, and how you can test and optimize your PPC efforts.

OPTIMIZING PAID SEARCH

This time we are looking at everything else you need to understand to help you make the most of your PPC activity. We will discuss the importance of Ad Rank and Quality Score and what you can do to improve both, and we will also explore the different targeting options and bidding strategies available to you. Finally, we will round the chapter off with a look at how you can optimize your PPC activity to ensure that this type of advertising gets you a great return on your investment.

WHO WILL SEE MY ADS?

So, you have created your ads, decided on your keywords and landing pages, and set the whole lot up in your Google Ads account. But how can you determine who is actually going to see your ads? As with any targeting you must think about your target audience. Who are your customers? Where are they based? What language do they speak? How old are they and how will other demographic factors affect their responses to your advertising?

Thankfully, Google provides a lot of different targeting capabilities you can implement to ensure your ads are being shown to the right people.

Google's location targeting capabilities range from entire countries to regions, cities, zip codes and even the radius around a location - like a certain distance around your business. You can also target by the number of potential users your ad will reach within a given area, or by people who have shown an interest in a particular location.

It is also possible to prevent your ads from showing in specific areas within your overall target. This would be useful to implement if you want to exclude certain zip codes from your ads for your home delivery service, for example.

Language is also a very important targeting consideration. Users' language preferences are determined using signals like browser settings and the language of their queries. This means that if someone's interface is set to French but they searching English, they'd be eligible to see ads in both French and English. To stay organized, It is best to create separate campaigns for each language that you choose to advertise in. Bear in mind that users can easily spot poorly worded copy, so always work with professional translators if you are going to create ads in languages that are not your native tongue.

Finally, demographic targeting allows you to target users by gender, age range, parental status, or household income. This can be very useful if you want to restrict your ads to specific segments or if your ads are for products like insurance, where millennials may have very different needs to customers over the age of 50.

So, location, language and demographic targeting are all offered by Google to help you target the right people. But there are a number of other targeting options that you may want to leverage.

In-market Audiences allow you to target predefined sets of users that Google believes are 'in the market' for various products and services - like computer parts, baby products or travel services. These audiences are selected based on their previous and current search queries. Customer Match gives you the option to upload lists of customer email addresses, physical addresses, or phone numbers to Google Ads. Where Google can match these details to the information it holds on a user, you can then use this option to target specific individuals from your lists.

Google also offers you the opportunity to remarket to customers who have previously visited your site. By linking Google Ads with your Google Analytics account, you can create lists of users with similar behaviors - like individuals who visited a specific page on your site, or every person who abandoned their shopping cart - and then upload these users to Google Ads for targeting purposes.

This option differs from Customer Match audiences, because with retargeting you do not know who the users are because tracking is done anonymously using cookies. However, it can be very effective because not only has this audience already shown a level of interest in your business but they are now using search queries that match your keywords, indicating that there should be a high chance of conversion if they see your ad.

Finally, Google also offers advertisers the opportunity to target audiences who display similar behaviors to those on your remarketing lists, but who have not yet visited your site. This is called 'Similar Audiences' and is an option that can significantly increase your reach to people who are likely qualified visitors but who may not be familiar with your business.

WINNING THE TOP SPOT ON THE RESULTS PAGE

We have discussed how you might decide on a budget for paid search activity and stressed the importance of allocating the appropriate amount to this type of advertising. But, as with all marketing activities, succeeding at paid search does not just depend on how much you are willing to spend.

When a user enters a search query, the search engine identifies which ads will be most relevant to that query based on the keywords and targeting parameters selected by the various advertisers. All ads deemed appropriate then go forward into an auction that decides which ads will appear on the results page, and the order in which they will appear.

Money alone will not win you that coveted top spot. This is because search engines want to avoid showing irrelevant or spammy ads to searchers and solely prioritizing the highest bidders would mean that advertisers would not need to optimize ads to their fullest extent - they would just need to spend the most money to appear at the top of the results page.

To help determine where ads place on the results page, Google uses a metric known as Ad Rank, which is calculated using a number of factors. One of these factors is Quality Score.

Quality Score is a real-time rating of the quality and relevance of your keywords, ads, and landing pages to a user's query. It represents Google's estimation of how well your ads meet searchers' needs. If Google views your ad as relevant to that search query, it will reward you with a high Quality Score which can help your ads to be shown higher on the results page.

Quality Score is calculated each time an ad is eligible for display. The calculation uses multiple factors, including the relevance of the search term to the Ad Group's keywords and the ad copy, the ad's click-through rate, the relevance of the ad's landing page and its bounce rate and your account's historical performance overall.

You can view your Quality Score for each keyword in Google Ads, although It is important to remember that this is simply an indication of how your ads rate. As Quality Score is determined in real-time, the Quality Score rating you will see in Google Ads is simply an average score, not your actual rating.

So that is Quality Score, and how It is calculated. But where does Ad Rank come in?

Ad Rank is a value that determines the position of an ad on the results page, and whether your ad will show up at all. It used to be determined using just two factors: the maximum bid price an advertiser was willing to pay for a click on their ad and the Quality Score of that ad. However, recently Google made changes to the algorithm that calculates Ad Rank, adding in a third component: ad extensions. Remember, ad extensions are additional pieces of information about your business, like your phone number or a link to a page on your site, which appear below your ad.

As well as using your maximum bid and your Quality Score to determine Ad Rank, Google now takes the "expected impact" of your ad extensions - and the format of those extensions - into account. Put simply, this means that using ad extensions is now pretty essential if you want to achieve a high Ad Rank and appear at the top of the results page.

Once ads are entered into the auction, each individual ad's Ad Rank is determined and then the available spots on the results page are given away, with the ad achieving the highest Ad Rank getting the top spot, the second highest getting the next spot and so on.

The calculation to determine Ad Rank occurs every time an ad is chosen for auction, so an ad's position on the results page might fluctuate depending on the variables in play at each auction. Your Ad Rank will vary, for example, depending on the context of a person's search and your competition in each auction – if other advertisers are willing to pay more than you, then your Ad Rank might be lower in some auctions.

Not only does Ad Rank determine where you place on the results page, but it can also affect the price you pay per click. To work out how much you pay for a click on your ad, Google takes the Ad Rank of the advertiser below you on the results page and divides it by your Quality Score. It then adds one cent or penny to that number and that is the price you end up paying per click. This means that not only should a higher Quality Score give you a better Ad Rank, but it may lead to you paying less for a click on your ad too.

No one outside of Google knows exactly how Quality Score is calculated, but we do know that click-through rate is the most important factor. If a user sees your ad and clicks through to your website, that is a clear indicator that your ad is relevant and useful to searchers and Google will reward you with a higher Quality Score and therefore a higher Ad Rank and lower costs.

At the heart of Quality Score is relevance, so if you are struggling to increase it, It is worth going back to your keywords. Do more research and discover new, more relevant keywords that you can include in your Ad Groups. Ensure your ad copy is tailored towards each Ad Group and your keywords

- if needed, split your Ad Groups out to ensure they are more specific to individual users' needs and search queries.

Finally, make sure your landing pages work for each ad and give searchers the information they are looking for, providing an optimal user experience right through from their initial search to - hopefully - conversion.

The next thing we need to take a look at is bidding strategies. There are two key types of bidding strategy you need to know about: manual bidding and automated bidding.

Manual bidding – also known as manual CPC (cost per click) – is very simple. You manually set the maximum price you are willing to pay per click, either at the Ad Group level or by individual keyword, and Google will bid for your keywords in auctions at the maximum bid price you set. The price you pay for winning at auction does not change - unless you manually increase or decrease it.

With automated bidding, however, you allow Google to automate your bid price based on the likelihood of your ad achieving a click or conversion. To determine this, Google uses machine learning along with data they hold on the searcher, such as their location, the device they are using and demographic data.

Automated bidding is designed to solve two pressing issues that advertisers come across when running paid search campaigns. First, how do advertisers know if their bids are high enough to compete for the most qualified searchers? And second, how do they know if they are bidding too high on clicks that just are not going to convert?

Automated bidding seeks to address these issues, because if Google can automatically change your bid price based on information it has on a searcher, then you should run less risk of over-bidding on unqualified clicks or failing to bid high enough for visitors who are likely to convert.

However, automated bid strategies do give you less control over your bid price, and they do mean you give Google itself a great deal of control over the price you pay fora click on your ad, so you should bear this in mind before you utilize automated bidding for all your paid search ads.

Within automated bid strategies are certain options that Google has termed 'smart bidding' strategies. These tend to be focused on optimizing for conversions or conversion value.

Currently, Google offers five smart bidding strategies...

If you have been using manual bidding for some time and want to step into automated bidding territory, Enhanced CPC (cost per click) is a good place to start. With Enhanced CPC, Google will change your manual bid based on the likelihood of achieving a sale or conversion. For clicks that seem more likely to convert, Google will raise your max bid, whereas it will lower your max bid for clicks that seem unlikely to convert. It is a good option if you are looking to increase your conversion or click-through rate, but it can lead to a higher cost per click than your maximum bid price, so you will need to have enough budget to sustain this approach.

Target Cost per Action (or CPA) is another smart bidding strategy, and aims to get you the most conversions possible, at or below a specific cost per action. It uses historic campaign information as well as information about the user performing the search to find an optimal bid price.

Target Return on Ad Spend - or ROAS - helps you to optimize for the value of each conversion, with bids set to achieve conversions at your targeted return on ad spend. Like Target CPA, Google will use historical data to maximize conversion value but rather than looking to achieve a specific cost per action, it aims to help you hit a certain return on your ad spend.

If you want to increase visibility at the top of the results page, Target Impression Share might be the strategy for you. It works by automatically setting bids with the aim of showing your ads somewhere on the results page. This strategy will allow you to dominate search results and will generally ensure that your ads will always be displayed if they match the search query. However, it can hit your budget hard, so you will need to have enough money to sustain it.

Finally, Maximize Conversions looks to give you as many conversions as possible within your daily budget. It is a useful strategy if you want to spend your entire budget, but are not too worried about how much you are paying to achieve each conversion.

There are also a couple of other automated options from which you can choose.

If you are trying to increase visits to your website, you might choose the Maximize Clicks bidding strategy. This simply looks to achieve the highest number of clicks possible and Google will let you place a cap on each bid, meaning you retain some control over the maximum amount you will bid on one click.

Finally, Maximize Conversion Value allows you to choose the value you want to maximize - like revenue - and Google will attempt to optimize your campaigns for conversions that are the most valuable for your company, while sticking to your daily budget.

If you are just starting out with PPC, It is advisable to begin with manual bidding. Then, as your experience grows, you can experiment with automated bidding. Switch some of your campaigns to automated strategies, and then compare the results with your manual bidding history to determine if Google's automated decision-making meets your needs.

As you monitor your campaigns, you might discover that there are certain instances where you are getting an increased number of clicks or conversions - for example, maybe you get better responses to your ads on mobile devices, in the evening, or on certain days of the week.

To capitalize on these instances, Google offers what are called bid adjustments. These allow you to increase or decrease bids based on certain criteria, and can be set for the overall campaign or at the individual Ad Group level. You can also combine more than one bid adjustment to achieve your goals. For instance, you might tell Google "increase bids by 10% on weekdays between 5pm and 7pm and increase by another 20% for mobile devices at these times".

Bid adjustments are powerful tools, but you should ensure that you always test for the best level of modification. Would increasing your bid adjustments from 10% to15% be worth the extra investment? You should also review your decisions relating to bid adjustments on a regular basis for changing conditions that might cause a previously effective adjustment to no longer benefit you.

TESTING AND OPTIMIZATION

Now you understand the different ways you can target your paid search ads, how the auction process works and the different bidding strategies you can employ to achieve your goals, there's one final thing to get your head around before you begin running your PPC campaigns: how do you know if they are working and, more importantly, how can you demonstrate that they are delivering a good return on your investment?

Needless to say, you must ensure that your advertising spend is generating results that support your business goals and justify your budget, and the good news is that there is a huge amount of data available to help you achieve this.

There are a number of KPIs you can use to find out how well your ads are performing. Impressions are the number of times your ads appeared in search results, regardless of the amount of clicks they received. If your goals include increasing brand awareness, impressions are worth keeping an eye on, as it means that searchers will have seen your product listing even if they did not click on it.

Clicks are another basic measure of your success - if your ads are not being clicked on, then something is not working for you! You should also check your click-through rate regularly: a high click-through rate indicates that your ads are persuasive to searchers, while a low click-through rate might indicate that while your ads are winning the auctions, they are not relevant to searchers' needs.

The whole point of PPC is to drive visitors towards a specific outcome, so the number of conversions you get from your ads is very important. Keep an eye on your conversion rate: a low conversion rate might indicate that your landing pages are not appealing to visitors, or that you need clearer calls to action.

To help you understand what you are spending to achieve each sale, the amount you are paying for each conversion should also be monitored. If your acquisition costs are higher than you would like, you could try adding negative keywords to your Ad Groups to improve the relevance of your ads, and remove any keywords that are clearly ineffective in generating conversions.

Finally, look at how much you are actually paying for every click on your ads - your cost per click - since It is not necessarily the same as what you bid. Keeping an eye on this means you can monitor your overall budget and reduce or remove bids for underperforming keywords.

Another metric you can use to determine how well your ads are performing is Return on Ad Spend, or ROAS. This is an important measure of whether the resources you are putting into your ads are worthwhile. It focuses on the ratio of ad spend to revenue and is calculated by dividing the total revenue made by your total costs. Your ideal Return on Ad Spend will depend on the financial situation of your business and your desired margins, but a common benchmark is a 4:1 ratio - $4 of revenue made for every $1 spent on advertising.

Using an effective combination of these metrics should give you a good idea of how your ads are performing, as well as giving you some clear direction about what needs changing in order to improve them. But, if you have been doing PPC for some time, you might want to get a bit more granular.

Perhaps your ads are performing well and you suspect that you might not actually need to be bidding so much – maybe you believe that you can bid slightly less and still end up near the top of the results page.

If this is the case, you might want to take a look at the 'top impressions' metric in Google Ads. This reports the number of times your ad was shown in the top paid spots on the results page. By evaluating what you achieve when your ads are shown in different positions on the results page, you might discover that slightly lower - and therefore cheaper - ad placements might be sufficient to meet your needs.

'Impression share' is another popular metric. Expressed as a percentage, it takes the number of impressions your ad actually received, and divides it by the number of times it was eligible to be shown. Eligibility is determined by a number of factors, like the targeting parameters for your ad, your bid price, and your Quality Score.

This can reveal interesting insights about your ad campaigns; especially if you are interested in finding out how you can better compete against rival brands on the results page. If your impression share is low, it suggests that your competitors are beating you in the ad auction, meaning that they probably have higher Quality Scores or bids (or both) and you will need to improve these to appear more often on the results page.

Finally, maybe you are losing impressions but you are unsure if this is due to the quality of your ad itself, or if you are simply not paying enough to appear on the results page.

The catchily titled 'impression share lost due to budget' metric can tell you where you are losing impressions because your budget is too low. If this is the case, you will need to either raise your bids or work on your Quality Score so that your Ad Rank increases.

Once you have identified areas where your performance is 'below par,' you can start testing variations of your current ads to figure out where you can make improvements by optimizing your ads, your landing pages, your targeting, and your bidding strategies.

For testing purposes, Ad Groups should contain more than one ad: your current 'master' ad and a number of alternative A/B test variants, where you can test different headlines, ad copy or extensions. You can even test which bidding strategies work best, what kind of targeting helps your ads perform best and which landing pages appeal most to visitors.

Once you have created variations on the ads that you want to test, Google offers two different choices for ad rotation.

Your first choice is to optimize your ad rotation, where Google will show a preference for the best-performing ad. Aided by Machine Learning, it will deliver the ad within the Ad Group that it believes will generate the best result. Any campaigns using 'smart bidding' will automatically default to this setting.

The other option you have is to choose not to optimize, but to rotate the different ad variations indefinitely - at least, until you decide to stop. This setting directs all of the ads within the Ad Group to be shown in turn, regardless of performance. This can be a good option if you want to see an unbiased long-term view of your campaigns, but continuously running low performing ads will waste your budget and could also mean you risk your Quality Score decreasing, which may affect your Ad Rank.

As you work to optimize the ads that appear on the results page, It is worth remembering that ads do not always result in an immediate conversion or sale. A visitor might see your ad but choose to continue with their research and return to your website sometime later once they have moved further along down the customer journey.

Sometimes, a buyer might have already been aware of your company and a buying decision that appears to come as a result of seeing one of your ads might simply be because your ad jogged their memory. You should also consider the possibility that users may well only be clicking on your paid ads because they appear higher up the page than any of your organic results.

These examples are just some of the reasons why you should not attribute all of your revenue to PPC, even though it may well appear to be the source of many of your conversions. You should factor in all of the resources and channels that have influenced a sale, rather than assuming that PPC is as successful as you think it is. This is called multi-channel attribution, and you can use Google Analytics to help you with attributing the credit to different channels throughout the customer journey.

That is all we have time for in this series of chapters. It is undoubtedly a powerful marketing tactic, but paid search requires patience and a lot of care if you wish to take full advantage of it.

Used effectively, it holds a lot of potential for businesses, so we hope that this guide has boosted your confidence and given you a good understanding of all things PPC - from setting up your Ads account, to demonstrating a return on investment. The rest is up to you...

GLOSSARY

Accelerated Mobile Pages (AMP) is an open source project which aims to improve the loading speed of mobile pages. It is essentially a stripped-down version of HTML – for example, JavaScript is not allowed and images do not load until you scroll to them.

Ad Auction is the process that happens with each search query. In the ad auction Google decides which ads will appear for each specific search, the order they will appear on the results page and how much each advertiser will pay for a click on their ad.

Ad Rank: The calculation that is performed to determine where your ad will position on the results page. Ad Rank is calculated using three factors: the ad's Quality Score, the maximum bid price the advertiser is willing to pay when a searcher clicks on their ad and the 'expected impact' of the ad's ad extensions.

Backlink is an inbound link to your site from some other site. Backlinks are by far the most significant off-site factor when it comes to optimizing for search.

Black Hat SEO refers to optimization techniques that breach search engine guidelines and which, if used, can result in your site being penalized or even removed from appearing in search results.

Branded Keyword is a keyword which includes the name of your business or organization. Likewise, a branded search query is a search which includes the name of your business or organization.

Breadcrumbs are navigational links that are displayed at the top or bottom of a page to help visitors and search crawlers navigate and understand a site.

Cloaking refers to a "black hat" technique in which the server distinguishes between actual human visitors and crawlers, producing a different version of the page for each with the aim of deceiving the search engine into indexing for content which is not reflected on the actual page.

Crawlers is an automated bot which searches through pages of websites, looking for clues about the subject of each one. Search engines then use this information to build their indexes.

Dwell Time refers to the amount of time visitors spend on a given site before returning to the results page.

Dynamic Serving is a type of site design in which the server detects the user's device type and returns content tailored to that device. Here, the URL for the site remains the same across devices, however the set of files served differs depending on the device.

Featured Snippet is a box that appears at the top of a search engine results page which contains the answer to the search question sourced from a webpage, and includes the webpage's URL and title.

Index is a huge database of information on billions of websites, which is used to evaluate the relevance of webpages to search queries.

Keyword is a word or set of words that is of particular relevance to a given website or page. Often, these will correspond (but may not be identical) to the search queries that generate traffic to the site or page.

Keyword Stuffing is a "black hat" technique in which a webpage is filled with keywords that are irrelevant, or keywords that are repeated so often that the content is difficult to read, in order to rank for keywords that the content does not actually reflect.

Long-Tail Keyword are keyword phrases which consist of several words. Likewise, a longtail search query is a search which consists of several words. These are usually created by adding modifiers to a central keyword, for example location or other specifics.

Non-Branded or generic keyword is a keyword which does not contain the name of a business or organization

Search Engine Optimization (SEO) is the subset of search engine marketing that focuses on improving visibility within organic, or unpaid, search results.

Search Engine Results Page (SERP) The search engine results page, often referred to as "SERP," is the page of listings that is displayed by a search engine following

Short-Tail Keyword is a keyword which only consists of one or two words. Likewise, a short-tail search query is a search which only consists of one or two words.

ABOUT JULIAN DELPHIKI

Julian Delphiki is a pseudonym, created to safeguard the integrity of his personal identity and ensure that the focus remains on transformative ideas rather than the individual. This philosophical stance permeates every aspect of his work, from his senior role in a renowned multinational company to his more private collaborations such as one-on-one executive coaching sessions.

For more than two decades, Julian has successfully navigated demanding environments in both well-established corporations and cutting-edge startups in pioneering eCommerce sectors such as fashion. This extensive journey has shaped him into a multifaceted professional whose expertise is not merely theoretical but firmly rooted in practical application. As a seasoned professional, he has honed his skills across diverse functions—ranging from managing complex projects to leadership and activation—consistently delivering results that reflect his unwavering commitment to the success of every initiative.

His strategic vision and adaptability have made him a pragmatic visionary, capable of understanding the needs of the market, businesses, and audiences alike. Beyond his corporate career, Julian is the founder and principal consultant of his own firm, where he channels this experience to help organizations of all kinds optimize their operations and achieve sustainable growth. His work in this space often spans digital marketing, online business, and, more broadly, business management and productivity.

Yet Julian's influence extends far beyond the executive committee. He is also a prominent figure in the realms of personal development and philosophical exploration. As a lecturer in various universities and business schools, he is also a dedicated coach, devoting his energy and passion to fostering personal growth. His coaching philosophy embraces a holistic approach, carefully intertwining personal development with philosophical introspection. This dual perspective enables him to delve deeply into the nuances of critical issues in the social sciences. With a genuine passion for empowering individuals to reach their fullest potential, Julian engages in inspirational and transformative conversations while offering practical tools to catalyze positive change in people's lives.

The fusion of Julian Delphiki's professional and personal spheres creates a truly unique mosaic of skills, knowledge, and a profound commitment to enhancing individuals, organizations, and society as a whole. His ability to bridge the strategic demands of the professional world with the deep self-knowledge required for personal growth provides an extraordinary lens through which to understand human behavior and psychology, the direction of businesses, and the evolution of society.

This interdisciplinary foundation makes him a compelling voice, capable of publishing thought-provoking books on a wide range of topics—united by his core mission of fostering growth and understanding in a complex world.

OTHER BOOKS BY THE AUTHOR

La abolición del trabajo. BLACK, BOB and DELPHIKI, JULIAN. 2024.

Maestros del hábito. DELPHIKI, JULIAN. 2023.

Modern philosophers. DELPHIKI, JULIAN. 2022

A modern hero. DELPHIKI, JULIAN. 2022.

Folkhorror volume I. DELPHIKI, JULIAN. 2022.

Ad tech and programmatic. DELPHIKI, JULIAN. 2020.

eCommerce 360. English edition. DELPHIKI, JULIAN. 2020.

eCommerce 360. Spanish edition. DELPHIKI, JULIAN. 2020.

Content marketing and online video marketing. DELPHIKI, JULIAN. 2020.

Digital transformation. DELPHIKI, JULIAN. 2020.

Optimizing SEO and paid search fundamentals. DELPHIKI, JULIAN. 2020.

Social media business. DELPHIKI, JULIAN. 2020.

Tales of horror and history. DELPHIKI, JULIAN. 2020.

Web Analytics and Big Data. English edition. DELPHIKI, JULIAN. 2020.

Analítica web y móvil. Spanish edition. DELPHIKI, JULIAN. 2019.

www.ingramcontent.com/pod-product-compliance
Lightning Source LLC
LaVergne TN
LVHW051243050326
832903LV00028B/2558